TO

___

FROM

___

DATE

___

MESSAGE

___

___

___

Living Balanced in a Tilted World

Christ -
Our living hope
Lynne

LIVING BALANACED IN A TILTED WORLD
Copyright © 2015 by Lynne Jordan
Published by Living Hope Ministries Today
Valparaiso, IN 46383
www.livinghopeministriestoday.com
ISBN: 978-0-9887651-4-6
Cover Illustration: Deanna Ehrhardt
Graphic Design: Bill Barrick

Unless otherwise noted all Scripture quotations taken from
the New American Standard Bible®,
Copyright © 1960, 1962, 1963, 1968, 1971, 1972, 1973,
1975, 1977, 1995 by The Lockman Foundation
Used by permission." (www.Lockman.org)

All rights reserved. No part of this publication may be produced, stored in a retrieval system, or transmitted in any form by any means – electronic, mechanical, digital, photocopy, recording, or any other except for brief quotations in printed reviews, without the permission of the publisher.

Living Balanced in a Tilted World

LYNNE JORDAN

LIVING HOPE MINISTRIES TODAY
www.livinghopeministriestoday.com
lynne@livinghopeministriestoday.com
Valparaiso, Indiana

TABLE OF CONTENTS

Dedication

Chapter 1 *Tilted 1*

Chapter 2 *Grounded by Grace 20*

Chapter 3 *Honesty's Healing Heart 39*

Chapter 4 *Identity Thieves 55*

Chapter 5 *Compassion's Counterweight 72*

Chapter 6 *Lingering 87*

Chapter 7 *Release 104*

Chapter 8 *Gratitude's Gravity 128*

Chapter 9 *Hope's Hunger 145*

Chapter 10 *Living with Vision 159*

Epilogue 169

Sources 171

Other Books by Living Hope Ministries Today 172

DEDICATION

To my mother,

Thanks for teaching me how to stand with strength. Living Balanced in a Tilted World requires that others have gone before us and taught us how to seek answers to difficult situations.

You have been that tutor. May God continue to use you to lead others toward finding hope in difficult circumstances.

Chapter 1
Tilted

Character cannot be developed in ease and quiet. Only through experience of trial and suffering can the soul be strengthened, ambition inspired, and success achieved.
Helen Keller

THE POTTER'S HAND

It was summertime, and a soft, warm breeze filled the room. The sun streamed through the window and onto my face. But I was numb. My face, a stream of tears. I didn't have answers. I couldn't even ask questions. All I could do was weep in disbelief.

I lay on my bed, confused, speechless, flooded with emotions I'd never experienced before. I kept trying to make myself understand, to rationalize through what felt like a nightmare from the darkest corners of my subconscious, but it was useless. Nothing in my life prior to this day could have prepared me for what I experienced that afternoon, only one day after it had happened.

I was in shock. Total, undeniable shock.

Somewhere in the background of my shattered world,

I heard a song. And as I lay on my bed, grasping desperately at threads of reality, these words broke through the mist of my utter confusion:

> *Take me, mold me, use me, fill me*[1]
> *I give my life to the Potter's hand . . .*

For a moment, I snapped back into consciousness. Music. I had put the CD on. A song I had never heard before. I listened closely. Momentarily, the fog of my grief lifted. The words continued:

> *Call me, guide me, lead me, walk beside me*
> *I give my life to the Potter's hand . . .*

The song lasted for only five minutes. Then it ended. I reached out from my bed and played it again. And again. And again. It was all I had in that moment.

Little did I know that it would become the first glimmer of hope since the phone call that changed my life forever.

THE CALL

Friday, July 27, 2007. It had every promise of a beautiful day. My oldest daughter was going to have her first "unofficial" date with her dad and me accompanying her as chaperones. My husband had taken the day off. I was mostly in high spirits, because I felt like it was a day in which memories were going to be made.

I remember doing normal things that morning: spending time with my husband, tinkering around at rummage sales. At one sale I found a worship CD I'd heard about. It was only two dollars, but the bargain-finder in me said no.

When I got back into the car, my husband said, "If you want it, then buy it! It's only two dollars."

Reluctantly, I went back and bought it. Half of me felt guilty for spending the money, while my other half sensed I had done the right thing.

We were all excited for that evening. When I got home, I set the CD aside, momentarily forgetting about it. Other things pressed on my mind. My daughter was going to take a skills assessment test at the local university. I was excited for her future but not about dropping her off. I needed to get things done at home before our night out.

The to-do list was a big one. Household chores. Planning for that evening. Maybe I would listen to that new CD.

But wait.

I remembered my parents. I needed to call them, but I didn't want to.

The night before had been messy to say the least. Two phone conversations with two parents, two perspectives, two lives, and one huge marital storm, forty-eight years on the precipice of disaster.

It was the last thing I wanted to deal with on a day that had started so perfectly. I didn't want to think about conflict—especially one between two people I loved so much. Part of me said it would probably blow over. The other part sensed that something was very wrong. I used to be confident that they would be able to weather their differences. This time I wasn't so sure.

It was one of those phone calls where you reach out, pick up, dial, then you hang up. It could probably wait until later, right? "Wrong," something inside me said. I wanted to ignore the pressing sense that I needed to check up on them, that they needed me to be there in the midst of this gale-force argument that was only getting worse. I couldn't do it.

And yet . . .

I dialed, almost without knowing it.

My mother picked up the phone. She sounded quiet and subdued.

I was confused. "Mom, is everything okay?"

She said something inaudible. Something was definitely not right. Then, on the other end of the line, I heard my father step into the room. Immediately, I understood.

"No, Glenn, please. Don't do that," my mother screamed.

Those words are seared into my memory. In a fraction of a second, the perfect day became the Last Day.

MOLD ME

Beautiful Lord, Wonderful Saviour
I know for sure, all of my days are held in Your hands,
crafted into Your perfect plan . . .

The words from the CD. The song that reeled me back into reality. In some cosmic way, my faltering two-dollar expenditure and that used CD were picking up the fragments of my life. The person that lay there in her bed, looking out the window into the impossibly beautiful summer's day, was nothing like who she'd been a day ago.

Some people say they are "broken." I was broken that day, but it was worse than that. I was beyond repair. It was as though I could see all the little, infinitesimal bits of my humanity spread out on the floor, where I'd held the phone on that Last Day.

Common sense was telling me that I would be like that for the rest of my life: broken into pieces too small and too many to puzzle back together.

But that song said something else.

Take me, mold me, use me, fill me
I give my life to the Potter's hand . . .

I was broken, yes. But that wasn't *my* last day.

LAST DAY

It was my father's.

My mother's pleas turned to screams.

I felt paralyzed in a way that only such a moment can make you feel. My mind raced. I yelled into the receiver, "Mom, what's wrong? *What's wrong?*" Was my father coming at my mother to harm her? She had shared with me the night before how he had uncharacteristically grabbed her arm. How could I stop him if she was being threatened?

Should I call 911?

No. I prayed. "Oh, Lord, please show me what to do" was all I could manage as I tried to understand what I could not see.

Then I heard him say it.

"Oh yes I am." Then the horrible explosion.

My father, a sixty-seven-year-old man, died by his own hand that July morning. Just like that, a life that was reasonably successful, a marriage of almost fifty years, and a father-daughter relationship were over. It all felt like a novel without a last chapter, though part of me still cannot believe that the story ended so abruptly, so tragically.

I will never be able to unhear that shot. I will never be able to unsee that scene. I will never be able to unlive that day. I could tell you in lucid detail the story of the days that followed. The procedures that had to be put in place. The investigations. The awful trip I took to the scene. The aching sense of loss that I still sometimes feel.

I will tell you about all of that and more.

But, first you have to understand something. Pay attention, because this is the beginning. This is what my story is about. This is why I wrote this book. This is who I am.

You see, my father's Last Day was also my First.

FIRST DAY

The words of the song "The Potter's Hand" recalled a verse from Jeremiah 18. "But the vessel that he was making of clay was spoiled in the hand of the potter," it says. "So he remade it into another vessel, as it pleased the potter to make."

That was me. Shattered, fractured, splintered, spoiled. I listened to the song again and again. As the summer afternoon became the summer evening, I felt something happening.

No. It was better than that. I *saw* something happening. I looked at my million-pieced self, pathetically scattered in every possible direction. Suddenly, the pieces rippled and melded together into the image of a cup. I was a cup. I was full of water. The weary and the wanting drank from me.

Then the cup shattered, pierced by a bullet and a scream with echoes of "Oh yes I am! OH YES I AM!" ripping at the fringes of my consciousness. But the vision broke, so I waited.

There I was again. Mud. Wet, slimy, incalculably fragmented, spinning on a wheel, being shaped by able hands. I would be a cup again.

But, wait. No. Not a cup. Not a cup at all—a deep, wide bowl able to hold three times as much water as the cup! My brokenness became plenty. My new self was foreign, but it was more than it had ever been before. I had been remade.

Suddenly I was back in my room. The CD had stopped spinning, the room was quiet. The night gently settled on the land outside my window.

I understood then. I may have been in a million pieces, but that didn't matter.

What mattered was what I was about to become.

And that was the end of my First Day.

Less than twenty-four hours after hearing my dad end his life, I had a firm hold on only one thing: that there was hope.

I'm not a wildly optimistic person. I don't appreciate sugarcoating. I like honesty, forthrightness, and blunt reality.

But on that day, I truly believed that there was a day in the future, no matter how far away, that I would not just be on my feet again; I would be a bedrock on which others could plant their own feet.

The way I saw it, my world had been thrown into chaos. That gunshot shook my universe, a grade 8.0 quake on my emotional Richter scale, rocking the foundations of my belief, my confidence, my stability, everything.

But something was going to happen. Even though my world had become shaken crooked, tilted beyond any semblance of normalcy, I had this absurd sense that I could attain—and even maintain—a sort of balance. The ground would never be level for me again, and I accepted that. But that didn't mean I couldn't compensate for it.

First, however, I needed to understand it.

TILTED

We all have different ways of coping. When something so shockingly unprecedented, so completely alien happens to us, we struggle like a drowning man to get to the surface of things. To breathe in the air of normality.

As I struggled in the viscous expanse of trauma and loss, I began to understand for the first time how *I* coped. Something inside of me was trying to rebuild my world.

It was a new world that came fresh with new visions, new concepts, and new ways to understand people, belief, and even God Himself. It was hard, but my mind slowly adapted. Along with this personal reformation came new terminology.

I used words and images—simple metaphors—to make sense of what I was becoming.

So it was that two words, two images found me one day and never left: tilt and balance.

I think if you were able to peruse the dictionary of my

new world, you might see a definition like this one:

Tilt: an event or circumstance that changes your life in such a completely devastating way, that it bears little to no semblance to what it was before. It forces you to question everything—your future, your relationships, your significance. It leaves you emotionally hunched over, mentally blinded, spiritually desperate, and often physically inept.

"Tilts" are not limited to death and trauma like I experienced. They can and do include:

- terminal or chronic diagnoses such as cancer
- the death of a spouse, parent, sibling, or child via war, suicide, or murder
- an accident
- rape
- abuse
- slander or gossip
- job loss
- divorce
- a financial crisis
- trials at your workplace
- the sudden loss of a friendship
- discovering that your child is experimenting with destructive vices

The list could go on.

I soon realized that a tilt is more than just an item on a list.

In the eye of my mind I could see an image of the tilted world: eerily askew, an oblique landscape made of twisted lines and jagged contours. If there were any clear paths at all, they never ran straight or level. It was a place of constant inclines and sharp slopes, scattered with obstacles that were either too enormous to conquer or constant and petty enough to be maddening. It was a spiritual inferno, a leech that fed off physical strength, an endless mental prison.

Anyone who travels in the tilted world is inevitably harrowed by a wellspring of crushing emotions. That much was obvious. But at the root of every obstacle, every slope, every twist in the path, one thing reigns supreme. It is a silent, secret destroyer, an enemy that often goes unseen.

It is despair.

I know that for a fact because, on the Last Day, I had come very close to succumbing to it forever.

LIVE AGAIN

Adopting, visualizing, and eventually understanding this idea of a tilted world helped me realize two vital things about the nature of chaos and suffering, not only in my life but in the lives of millions who suddenly and jarringly find themselves trapped inside tilted realities.

They are, in brief, as follows:

1. When you are caught in the center of loss, pain, trauma, despair, etc., it's *not* the time to try and figure out how you got there. You have to decide soon whether you are going to stay frozen—or step forward, despite the shock. Decisions made in the moment can and *will* impact your future well-being. Are you going to obsess over how dramatic and permanent the damage seems to be, or will you surrender, allow change to change you, redirect you, reshape you?

2. If you truly believe in a restorative power that is beyond you, ahead of you, and bigger than the present moment—as I do—you are going to have to decide whether or not you actually *trust* that there can be hope, despite the landscape ahead of you. Every day, tilted world or not, you have to decide whether what you believe in is worth acting on. Let's be honest, it's not hard to see where people really place their trust, is it? Just look at the choices they make.

These were not easy things to accept. I was still grieving. I still felt the immense emptiness of loss, betrayal, sorrow beyond measure. But something inside told me that if I didn't act, if I didn't trust, if I didn't try to understand the tilted world, I would never truly live again.

BALANCED

Charles Blondin was a circus performer who amused himself and thousands of spectators by stretching out a steel cable across Niagara Falls and lithely strolling across it like he was taking a Sunday walk.

Often he'd perform this daring feat during high winds. Often he'd do it without a safety net. He'd go from walking to dancing—even running—across the cable in a single performance. When he felt especially cheerful, he'd fill a wheelbarrow with bricks and push it effortlessly back and forth on the cable.

But he wouldn't stop there.

One day, knowing he had the crowd's full attention, Blondin asked, "How many of you believe that I could push a man across the wire in the wheelbarrow?"

The crowd raised its hands without reserve. Even if they didn't believe it, they still wanted to see it.

Then Blondin asked the kicker question, "Would one of you please volunteer to be that man?"

Every hand dropped.

The acrobat smiled to himself. There was, apparently, a big difference between belief and trust.[2]

As I lay in bed on that First Day, I decided something absolutely unprecedented. I decided that I could actually *trust* God to safely take my life and repurpose it, if that's what He wanted to do. My belief broke the bounds of my frailty and became a devout and earnest assurance in the sovereignty of a holy God who has a flawless history of making and keeping promises.

SO IT WILL STAND

I've taught Sunday school for over thirty years. Out of all the subjects I've addressed in my classes, the sovereignty of God has been one of the most rewarding and the most challenging. In those first days of anguish, verses from my lessons began to materialize from corners of my subconscious, little gifts and sweet reminders of a presence infinitely higher and wiser than my own.

> *The Lord of hosts has sworn saying, "Surely, just as I have intended so it has happened, and just as I have planned so it will stand . . . For the Lord of hosts has planned, and who can frustrate it? And as for His stretched-out hand, who can turn it back?"*
> *Isaiah 14:24, 27*

> *My purpose will be established, and I will accomplish all My good pleasure . . . Truly I have spoken; truly I will bring it to pass. I have planned it, surely I will do it.*
> *Isaiah 46:9–11*

> *I am He, and there is no god besides Me; it is I who put to death and give life. I have wounded, and it is I who heal, and there is no one who can deliver from My hand.*
> *Deuteronomy 32:39*

As hard as it was to accept, I realized that the moment my dad placed the gun to his head and pulled the trigger was the same moment I was rushed into the sovereign agenda of a God who was going to re-create me. I belonged to Him, and there was nothing, no one, no circumstance that could hold back the hand of this loving God. A God I trusted. *He* had planned my life—not me, not my father. And *He* would accomplish His great work even through the painful months that lay ahead.

Somehow, as I rested my head on a tear-soaked pillow, the summer night outside marking the end of that First Day, I rested assured. God was asking me to trust Him. I chuckled inside as I saw myself in that crowd before Blondin, the tightrope walker, raising my hand. "I'll get in the wheelbarrow," I said, almost out loud. "I trust You."

Pastor and speaker Andy Stanley writes that "convictions eliminate options."[3] In that moment I felt like God was telling me, "Consider your options. Do you simply believe in Me, or do you trust in Me *with conviction*?" Surrendering to the pain in that moment, I threw my arms up and said, "God, I trust You. Take me. Remake me. Use me for whatever purpose You intend. I surrender."

Since then, I've come up with another word, another image. It's the antithesis to "tilted" and at its heart is the surrender that became the first step in my journey to renewed hope: balanced.

It escapes a brief definition, because it's not just about a moment or an idea. It's a way of life. A mind-set. A worldview.

And it's exactly what this book is about.

LIVING BALANCED IN A TILTED WORLD

The chapters that follow are my story.

But more than that, they are what I hope to make *your* story as well.

Recovery is far from simple. The tilted world is not given to explaining itself or making the journey through suffering easier. But I sincerely believe in a few simple things.

1. The sovereignty of God and undeniable truth of His loving purpose for our lives through Jesus Christ;

2. The capability of every individual who has experienced "tiltedness" to experience and master emotional, psychological, and spiritual balance;

3. The power of an intentional, change-oriented mind-set that can and will lead not only to restoration but to powerful transformation.

This was my great discovery: pain is a gift, the tilted life itself, a blessing. Crisis, trauma, loss, and grief are the agents of the blackest kinds of pain humanity has ever suffered. But they have also been some of the greatest catalysts for healing, personal change, great achievement, and otherwise impossible freedom.

You see, pain forces us to ask meaningful questions, to challenge our belief. It drains distractions away until we can see the foundations our lives have been built on and the means by which those lives are held together. Through pain we can see where complacency has replaced resolve, where comfort has replaced conviction, and where stagnation has replaced purpose.

Living balanced in a tilted world means more than just getting by. It means more than just regaining your footing. It's a call to use pain, not as a crutch or an excuse, but as a springboard to a life lived to its full potential. God is as active as He's ever been, and right now He's in the business of making weakness into strength, frailty into leadership, fear into courage, and hopelessness into a beacon of hope. Pain is His tool, tiltedness His workshop, and we are His workmanship.

It's not going to be easy. I know. It wasn't easy for me.

Before you is a call to break free from the incorrect and sometimes unfair expectations of family, friends, false beliefs, and self-imposed standards. Embracing stillness, relinquishing any worry about how things will turn out, and understanding the difference between influence and personal control is hard. Identifying false trust and debunking the lies of a sugarcoated faith is even harder. But until we separate our ideas of how the world expects us to change from the truth of how God wants to change us, we will never be able to become truly balanced.

Romans 5:5 says that "hope does not disappoint." That's the reason you and I are here. I learned how to find hope in the midst of pain. You may be searching for hope, wondering what hope is, or even trying to find a way to explain to someone else that hope can never truly be lost. Pain isn't beyond our understanding, and more importantly, it's never beyond the power of Christ's sacrifice on the cross. If you're willing to begin with that assumption, to believe that hope is attainable and that God is its sole architect, then we can begin this trek through the tilted world together. If not, I encourage you to be brutally honest with yourself and consider this: if hope does not come from God, and this world is full of pain, then where *does* it come from?

With God's help, I'm going to reach out through the pages of this book and take your hand. Even though a day does not go by that I miss my father, that I grieve his loss, that I feel the ache of the scar that Last Day left me with, I am standing firm. I am balanced. I am a testament to the transformative thinking that comes with trust in a God who is drawing us to Himself through all circumstances, even the dark ones.

I'm reaching out to you, asking only two things:

First, let me help you. Don't put this book down.

Second, once you too become balanced, reach out, find another hand, and begin the process again.

God wants to help you, but He also wants you to be an agent of His promise that living balanced in a tilted world is not just about possibility—it's about destiny.

Living balanced is a call to use pain, not as a crutch or an excuse, but as a springboard to a life lived to its full potential.

Chapter 2
Grounded by Grace

Your worst days are never so bad that you are beyond the reach of God's grace. And your best days are never so good that you are beyond the need of God's grace.
Author Unknown

THE STORY

I love June in the Midwest. The harsh winter is long gone, the unpredictability of spring weather has abated, and the hot and sticky Indiana summer has yet to arrive. Everything is near perfect in June.

June of 2007 was no exception. I remember one morning when I stared out at the green grasses cloaking the countryside around my house. I breathed deeply, and the season tingled inside my lungs. Without using words or thoughts, I thanked God for life—just in my being and smiling.

It was my daughters' birthdays. We threw a joint party for them that year, inviting family over for an evening. Schedules were laid aside, priorities rearranged, *our* lives put on hold for the celebration of our daughters' lives.

I was acting hostess that night. Fueled by my love of the season and my deep thankfulness for the occasion, I ran in and out of the house. Dessert here, conversation there, dishes there. A cake. A song. Nothing was amiss . . .

. . . until my father called me aside. "I want to talk to you and your siblings in private," he said and walked outside. It seemed mysterious, to say the least, but I complied. I pulled a couple of chairs out to the porch. My father asked the other guests to stay inside.

That's how I found myself gathered with my siblings and my father on that June evening, listening to a story. A story that's still hard to accept as truth.

I remember my father sitting there. He seemed more relaxed than usual, more hesitant than I ever remembered. He seemed old, worn by years of hard life. Yet, the way that he looked at each of us was tender, even peaceful. That night, he wasn't the strong, sometimes harsh man I knew. I could tell he wanted to speak but didn't know where to start. He faltered. We looked at each other, confused. Then he began.

LOOKING INSIDE

"I'll do it," I said, trying not to show apprehension. "I don't want you to have to see that. I'll look." I tried to sound stronger than I felt. My mom needed that more than anything.

The funeral home needed a simple decision from us: open casket or closed. It was a decision I never imagined I'd have to make but one that I didn't want to burden my family with. I looked apprehensively toward the visitation room. The hallway loomed ahead of me. I couldn't walk down it and through those doors. I couldn't. But I had to. For Mom, for me, for everyone.

I had never been more frightened, more horrified to see anything in my life than I was to see what was behind those doors. But I needed closure. I needed to be sure beyond a shadow of a doubt that this was really happening.

So I walked, driven in a quest for answers and dreading what those answers would be.

The doors opened. The room was appropriately cold and empty. Ahead of me, the casket was open—waiting for me, it seemed. Daring me to find out the truth. I wanted to scream. I wanted to slam the lid closed in defiance, proving through my utter denial that my father was *not* dead, that my life had *not* been torn to shreds, that everything was normal. The coroner, the funeral home, the police report, the mourners at our home. They were all liars and lunatics! My father was not dead! He couldn't be.

He couldn't be.

In the same moment, grief and weakness hit me like a train. I wavered at the doors, weakness in my knees, blood draining from my face. Two colossal forces, denial and devastation, dueled inside me. I knew that seeing his face would somehow undo me—drive me insane, at the least. Seeing him like that, like I had never seen him before, would rip me from the glimpse of hope I had found in the midst of despair days earlier.

Why, all of a sudden, were the Potter's hands so absent?

I wanted to spare my family from the horror of what may be inside that casket. But nothing could keep me from being enveloped by it myself. For a moment, I had to become the nurse who had done postmortems, who had been there with the dying and the dead. I was strong enough.

I convinced my legs to walk to the casket.

I forced myself to look inside.

DID HE HAVE A NAME?

"He died," my father said. I heard it through a haze of confusion.

"It just started out as a fight. One man in a quarrel with another. But others joined in." He faltered. "I joined in. Only half of us knew what we were actually doing. It was dark. Most of us were drunk. There was a mob mentality about the whole thing." He shook his head. Then, finally, he looked up at us, met our eyes, and spoke. "To this day I don't know if it was my fist that finished him. I don't know. I don't . . ." A choke stifled him.

He was quiet then. He took a deep breath in and let it out in a sigh. It was the closest to a religious confession that my father had ever come. Later, we all agreed we felt like his priest, listening as he absolved himself of guilt with this overripe penitence.

I looked to my siblings for answers or understanding glances, but they were just as confused as I. I began to wonder what else I didn't know about this man I called my father. At the same time, I couldn't help but picture that awful scene. My father and other dark-faced men beating and bruising and breaking another human being, mindlessly ending a life. *What was the man doing there that night?* I wondered. *Did he have a family? Was there an investigation? A trial? Did he have a name?*

But I didn't dare speak. The air on the porch became like fragile glass that would break if we did anything but listened.

My father finished his story as he gazed out into the summer night, seeing, I imagined, his past and its dark but inextinguishable memories. He looked like he wanted to be at peace.

Perhaps he was for a moment, as we awkwardly thanked him for being honest and returned to the candles and the cake and the birthday songs.

I'll talk to him about it later, I thought afterward. And though the story of the dead man haunted me, I was confident that—because it was in the past and finally out in the open now—my father would recover in his own way.

I never had that talk.

MY FATHER'S WORLD

How can I describe what I saw?

There was the final, incontrovertible proof. My father. Still. Cold. Silent. Not alive. His head was sickly swelled where the bullet hit. Not ugly but disproportionate, strange and unreal in its every contour. Horribly uncanny. I could see the putty where the artists had done their best. Here was my evidence. The verdict was final.

Then it happened.

I had expected horror, fear, repulsion, and the unforgiving torture of loss. I had expected to be slammed by a tidal wave of grief, to feel like a rowboat on the back of an immense and violent sea. I had expected to be utterly lost in a strangling mist of confusion and disbelief.

But I could feel one thing and one thing only.

I looked at him, my father whom I loved and who had

loved me. In the lines of his face I saw the ghosts of every expression he ever wore: joy, anguish, victory, love, anger, contentedness, worry. They all passed in a matter of moments like a picture of his life painted perfectly and then dissolved into dust. What was left, oh! What was left was more than human.

Could you understand if I told you that my father was never more alive to me than in that moment? I could feel something take hold of me—a power greater than life itself. It showed me not a body but a human being who had been broken, hurt, left helpless and devastated by a force that had crushed him underfoot.

Suddenly I realized where I was. The tilted world. It was darker than usual and crooked as ever. But it was not mine.

It was my father's.

I saw him there–crumpled, weak, and hopeless. Small. Naked. Alone. Pleading in something akin to a whisper, "Help, help me!" as he lay alongside the jagged path, wounded, unable to rise.

I stooped beside him, took his head in my hands, and heard myself say again and again through my tears, "Oh dad. Oh dad!"

Some say that because the dead cannot feel compassion, the living cannot give it to them.

But that's a lie.

Everything in his face told my father's story from beginning to end. A story about a man starving for compassion, love, forgiveness, and grace. A man who had died not by his own hand but from a cruel emaciation that, after it had deprived him of all his hope, had stolen his life as well. Behind his strength in life was a constant, lurking dread that he was worthless, hopeless, valueless, loveless. And when I saw that clearly, I wanted more than anything to become the very thing he needed, to show him a compassionate grace so total and complete that it would undo the stranglehold of his every care.

As I stood there beside the casket, and as my soul knelt beside the road in that world beyond, I felt overwhelming, unfettered compassion for my father. Plus, I knew that in some way, he felt it too. I didn't beg him to come back. I didn't curse his leaving. I didn't demand answers. I just softly said to him, "Oh, Dad. I love you."

I did. I always will.

I fixed myself in that moment, weeping. I didn't look away from my father's face. I didn't let him go. In the silence, through my tears, both in that room and out of it, I was saying a long good-bye, knowing that was our moment. The last moment. Daddy and daughter. Together.

I cherished it.

LIKE SCARLET

Every day, people are drowning in guilt. Amid the storm of revelations and realizations that I felt that day in front of the casket, my father's story of the bar fight and the dead man came back to me.

"Was that what my father took a bullet for?" I found myself asking hours after the incident. At the casket, there was no doubt in my mind. His guilt had torn him apart, starting in his heart and working its way up to his thoughts and, ultimately, into the finger that pulled the trigger.

It may sound strange, but I loved him all the more for that. Not because I felt trivial pity for him but because I saw what he had so desperately wanted and needed in his own life: grace.

My father's past has helped me plan my future in ways I never could have imagined. The story of his guilt has helped me shape my understanding of forgiveness. The story of his death has taught me the value of life in Christ.

The words of the old hymn never rang more true to me than they did that year.

Grace, grace, God's grace,
Grace that is greater than all our sin . . .[1]

It's a simple but central theological principle—an idea about who God is. God forgives. He is just, but in His justice and sovereignty and holiness, He is forgiving on a scale that we can only begin to comprehend.

We claim to hate it when people give each other labels such as liar, unfaithful, lustful, greedy, addict, whore, rapist, thief, gossip, slanderer. But we never know why we hate it. Why it makes us cringe.

It's true that, even if these labels sum up what we have done, they don't sum up who we are. We are God's. And belonging to Him gives us an identity that reaches beyond action and into purpose. Through the power of grace and through forgiveness, God can restore any misappropriated identity out there. We just have to be humble enough to ask.

My father wanted to believe in his own strength more than he did God's. I'm not assuming. I know, because that night on the porch, he left us with a sobering confession. "I cannot forgive myself," he said, hoping that telling someone else would at least allow him to feel momentarily cleared of guilt. He made the mistake that so many people make. He tried to forgive himself without asking for God's forgiveness.

I understand that it's important to feel as though we owe it to ourselves to find a sort of inner peace in the wake of sin, guilt, and devastation. I'm not saying that's a bad thing altogether. But it's utterly insufficient.

Forgiveness is something we reach out and accept. It's God's offer to restore us, not an opportunity to restore ourselves. God extends that offer in the most supernatural and perfectly sufficient gesture of love the universe has ever known—the death and salvation of Jesus Christ.

"Grace, Grace . . ." The song plays an infinite loop in the back of my mind. *"God's grace, Grace that will pardon and cleanse within . . ."*

I wish that my father hadn't fallen prey to the despair of a life lived desperately grasping for that grace.

But I have new eyes now. Before the casket closed, before the day ended, I felt the weight of a grace-starved world on my back, a sea of people drowning in a sea of pain. My good-bye to my father became my cry to them.

"I love you," I cried out to them. "I love you!"

MILK

There's a little boy. He's three years old. He sees his dad eating cookies in the living room and gets an idea.

He gets a chair from the dining room and drags it to the kitchen, leaving a path of parallel scratches on the new wood floor. The chair gets stuck on a cabinet. He pulls until the chair comes loose, but not before it leaves an ugly gash in the face frame.

The boy finally gets to the counter. He retrieves a glass.

It's a bit large and a bit wet. He drops it into the kitchen sink. It shatters, the pieces falling into the garbage disposal. That's okay. He gets another one and climbs down from the chair, knocking it over in the process.

The refrigerator handle is above his head. He reaches up, opens the door, and looks for the milk. It's on the top shelf. He uses the inside of the fridge as a step and hauls the milk—and several other food items with it—down. Setting the glass on the ground, he makes his first attempt at transferring the milk from gallon to glass. It works. Well, sort of. The floor gets its fair share of milk too.

But now the hard part is done. The boy takes the glass in both hands and dashes to the living room, milk sloshing wildly onto the carpet in his wake. He runs up to the couch and smiles triumphantly, holding out the milk for his father to take.

The man looks at his son and the glass. A look of realization falls on his face. He turns, cookie in hand, and sees the chaotic mess that used to be a tidy kitchen. He looks at the boy, sopping wet with milk, smiling up at his daddy, holding out the glass. The father doesn't need to think about what to do next.

He scoops the little three year old up, glass and all, and hugs him, smothering him with kisses. The boy laughs a clear, ringing sound of pure joy.

"Thank you!" says the father. "I'm so proud of you!"

Then, together, they eat the cookies and drink the milk, the kitchen forgotten.[1]

There are days I wish my dad could have seen *his* Father reaching out in a gesture of embrace. Willing and ready to forgive. But the ruin was overwhelming. My dad succumbed to it.

He didn't have to. The forgiveness of God is light-years beyond our biggest scratches, gashes, breaks, and spills.

LET US REASON

We lead messy lives. Sometimes we are the cause of our own mess. Sometimes it's out of our hands. Regardless, messiness leaves stains. Indelible marks of mud that time won't wash away.

The stains eventually get to us, no matter how strong we think we are or appear to be. We are repulsed by them, afraid of them, embarrassed by them. We try to rub them out with whatever the world promotes as the antidote, the cleanse-all solution to any stain.

What we don't understand is that we're not just stained—we're tilted. Sure, the blotches and spots may be abundant, but they're nothing compared with the fact that our lives themselves have been altogether reconfigured. When we miss the point, we miss out on grace. We give in to self-loathing, finger-pointing, covering up, and playing games with ourselves and others.

It's a cycle that leads to depression, anxiety, and slow and sometimes silent self-destruction. It's only a matter of time until we do one of two things:

1. Succumb to that self-destruction.

2. Look for help.

Help can come from innumerable sources, such as honesty, relationship, love, change of pace, etc. But it originates in one person. Jesus Christ.

God once said to the nation of Israel through a prophet named Isaiah, "Come now, let us reason together . . . though your sins are like scarlet, they shall be as white as snow; though they are red like crimson, they shall become like wool" (Isaiah 1:18 ESV). He goes on to promise that if His people remain obedient and willing, He will bless them. It's nothing short of remarkable that a holy God would be willing enough to meet us here, in the middle of our tilted worlds, bearing forgiveness and grace to people who are desperate and in need of this cleansing. A people who cry out for the wounds they bear to be erased, or at minimum barely noticeable. *Grace. Grace. God's Grace. Grace that is greater than all my sin.*

He stoops down to us as we kneel on the barren road. He puts a comforting hand on our shoulder and says "I—

yes, I alone—will blot out your sins for my own sake and will never think of them again" (Isaiah 43:25 NLT).

Our throats ragged from calling out for help, we look up to Him, into the very eyes of grace. Faintly, we wheeze the only thing we can manage. "Yes."

He puts a steady hand under our arms and lifts. We're on our feet.

Suddenly, the stains don't matter anymore.

The choice we make in the moment that God shows us grace in the midst of sin and brokenness is a vital one. He promises to forgive if we ask for forgiveness. To help if we admit we need it. To blot out the stains if we stop indulging in them. To bring balance if we recognize we are incapable of leveling out the tiltedness ourselves.

GROUNDED

"I love you!" I shout to the multitudes. I said earlier that I saw them drowning, but let me tell you what I really see. Forgive me if the image is harsh.

I see a million people with a million loaded guns. I hear "Oh yes I will!" a million times over. My heart beats a million times a second, waiting for the shots to shatter a million lives.

I see a million desperate hearts that feel worthless, unloved, starving for hope. I hear a million voices shouting, "Love me! Look beyond my stains. Look beyond my guilt. Help me through this tilted world! I'm giving up. I need you! Love me!"

The world, friend, is incalculably more desperate than you or I can imagine. In the midst of our own pain, we are obligated to realize that most people have no idea what grace even is, much less how to embrace it. There's a reason why Christians say the world is lost outside of Christ.

I cannot help but hear my own father reiterate this from the grave at times. "Lynne," he says, "love them as they are. Live to show others the power of grace. Help them understand redemption. Weep for them as you did for me. Meet them on their road through pain. Give everything you have to get to them. Be with them, and never let them go. Be strong where I couldn't be. Be love where I could not find it. Be compassion where I never knew it. Be grace to a graceless world."

I'd like to say that it's been easy for me to respond with enthusiasm and a concerted effort to show and give grace to everyone I meet. But it hasn't been.

How am I supposed to respond to suicide? How am I supposed to turn a story of loss into a message of grace? Trust me when I say that I haven't always had the answers to those questions.

Time and trust have changed me. I've realized that navigating this tilted world of mine means I'll need firm footing and a good guide.

So, to put it simply, grace has been my footing and Jesus my guide. Not as a last resort but as an only choice. When I stood at the casket, I acknowledged that for the first of many times.

Let's talk about you for a moment. Whether you're struggling to achieve balance or have already, you should consider a few simple principles:

1. Sin is a given. But that's what forgiveness is for. Despite our guilt, despite what has happened to us, God can and will forgive, heal, and restore.

2. Grace is firm ground. Stumbling through tiltedness is inevitable, but falling is optional. God's grace is constant and pervasive. It's a durable, unbreakable force—not a fancy way of wistful thinking.

3. You can choose. God doesn't force people in one direction or the other. He gives us free will, and that means we can either experiment with our own frailty or we can be confident in Him. That's all there is to it.

To be grounded in grace means to live a lifestyle of grace—both on the receiving and the giving end of the process. The devastation that life brings our way is hard, but grace transcends that. We need to recognize that even though sin is vying for dominion by perpetuating devastation, grace is still "greater than all our sin." How can we be assured of this?

Well, for starters, Scripture makes it blatantly clear when it says, "He who began a good work in you will perfect it until the day of Jesus Christ" (Philippians 1:6) and "The Lord . . . is patient toward you, not wishing for any to perish but for all to come to repentance" (2 Peter 3:9). Perhaps most famously and most truthfully, Christ makes the purpose of grace flawlessly clear when He declares that "God so loved the world, that He gave His only begotten Son, that whoever believes in Him shall not perish, but have eternal life" (John 3:16).

To those who believe in the truth of these timeless promises, who trust Christ's power and His person to pick us up off the pavement and teach us to walk with grace beneath our feet, what are we waiting for? Let Him do His work. Be an emissary *for* that work.

READY TO BEGIN

It was hot. The heat of the July sun bore down on the procession. I watched sweat drip off the faces of the cemetery workers as they set up and climbed the scaffolding to place the casket into the mausoleum. As I watched them slide the box in and seal the compartment shut with metal rivets, I knew that my grace would never be able to get through those marble walls, past the cold coffin, and reverse death and time. But God was there, in the heat of the day, in the quiet of the graveyard, standing, arms wide and welcoming. I saw the tomb close, but I felt the reassuring presence of grace surrounding me like a cool breeze.

My dad's life was God's. I went home from the funeral, remembering everything: the talk on the porch, the open casket, the song, grace, hope, and so much more.

It was hard to know what the days ahead would bring, but I knew one thing now. The fierceness of the love of God, the sheer strength of grace, the freedom from guilt and shame—all of this was more than just an exercise in experience.

I was beginning a journey, an adventure, a new life in which God was going to make me an entirely new person.

By the grace of God, I was ready to begin.

Living balanced means to be grounded in grace both on the receiving and the giving end of the process.

Chapter 3
Honesty's Healing Heart

Your joy is your sorrow unmasked.
Kahil Gibran, The Prophet

TWO KNOCKS

Getting out of bed was hard.

Numbness settled in a day after my father died. As much as I wanted to be strong, I found myself fumbling through my morning—body on autopilot, mind disorganized, spirit crushed. I was rigid and disabled in every way, like an advanced Parkinson's patient struggling through simple thoughts as though they were complex word games.

My dulled senses strained to get me out of my bedroom and to my recliner, where I sat and stared, succumbed to the weight of emptiness.

Somewhere in the ragged corners of my consciousness, I heard a noise. A rapping. A knock at the door. This was the last thing I wanted to hear. *I don't have the energy to see anyone, much less to actually get out of this chair*, I thought.

Please, whoever you are, go away.

My husband answered the door.

I wanted to retreat into myself. I didn't need whatever pity my visitor was there to pass on. I knew there was hope in the future, but it was too soon. I felt as though I needed the rawness of the moment, though for what I couldn't say. Sympathy, the recognition that I was emotionally and spiritually torn to pieces, was what I knew I needed, but it was not what I wanted.

But I didn't have a choice.

Suddenly an arm wraps around my shoulders. My visitor, an old and very dear friend, isn't an intruder. In an instant, I began weeping. I don't remember what I said, only that all the grief-induced pseudo-intoxication of that morning narrowed down to wails, screams, and much-needed tears.

There was calmness about letting go, of relinquishing my grasp on preconceived notions that, to deal with pain, you had to first bury it deep inside you, to get over it and hope for things to get better. In a moment that only a friend can create, I faced myself as though in a mirror and accepted the ragged, torn, disheveled, lost, and hurting soul that I was. It was okay. And my friend made that clear to me.

Maybe it was coincidence. Maybe it was God making things clear to me. Maybe it was a fluke.

That same morning, there was another knock.

At first I thought heaven had sent another comforter. But this time, I had a very different conversation in which, to make a long story short, I was told to get a hold of myself. I won't say her name, of course, but I still remember that encounter clearly. Because, I was on the fence. I knew by the ruling emotional stoics in society that I should be composed in the midst of my loss, but I knew that my anguish was more genuine than a pretense of keeping it together.

Who was I supposed to be in such a situation? *What* was I supposed to be?

THE SWIMMING POOL

It's easier to hide the truth.

I remember a certain day in my childhood when I stood in my swimsuit, ready to rush out the front door. I had waited for this day ever since I knew our neighbors had a pool. To splash into the cool water on a sun-soaked afternoon seemed to me the very apex of high living. When I finally got the invitation, I didn't hesitate to grab my sandals and a towel as I made a beeline for the front door.

My mother stopped me before I put a foot out the front door. "No!" She insisted, almost worried, a little fear in her eyes, "Honey, you can't go swimming."

Dumbstruck was the only thing I could be. "Why?" As I asked out loud, I realized inwardly that my dream now faced an insurmountable opposition: Mother's final word.

Maybe I was too young to understand or to connect meaning to what had happened a day or so before. But I remember it today. My father's set face. Me lying there, defenseless. The leather belt in his hands. The lump of fear in my throat.

He was a strong disciplinarian, a man who believed that harsh punishment had proven results. So there I was, helpless, on the receiving end of a whistling belt buckle, wincing under the pain, trying to be stoic about it because I knew that's what my father would want.

I don't remember the offense. I didn't remember it when my mother answered my question a few moments later. "Because we don't want the neighbors to think your dad beat you."

Innocently, as I put the towel back and got dressed, I thought to myself, "But isn't that what he did?" I may have momentarily forgotten, but the purple and yellow blotches on my legs had not.

I accepted with reserve the unfortunate truth as I looked out the window at the shimmering bright-blue pool water across the street. *It was easier to hide the truth.*

HOW SHOULD I RESPOND?

"You've got to get a hold of yourself."

The words were jarring, harsh. But I realized I had a

choice now. There wasn't anyone telling me I couldn't step out the front door and expose the reality of the situation. Besides, what had happened was already laid bare before the world. Even though only a day had passed, the news of my father's suicide reached out, tendril-like, to the community. Only one thing remained to be seen. How would *I* take it?

I wish I could say I told the second visitor to leave me alone. I wish that I hadn't sat in stunned silence, donning that stoicism my father had worshiped and she demanded. I wish I hadn't swallowed my pain and played it safe. In the end, it was easier to hide. Not for me, for her.

Even after both visitors had left, one reminding me of the power of a stiff upper lip and the other comforting me with pure, sweet, loving words, insisting that hiding will only make things worse, I felt beat, knocked down. This time an emotional buckle had struck me.

The bruises had won this round.

I staggered back into a mire of pain.

SMILING DEPRESSION

The reality is this: in the end, even when there's no way to avoid pain, honesty about the *cause* of pain and its existence is the first step to freedom *from* it.

Truth is freedom, healing, and strength. I see it as a

salve for raw, open wounds. It opens dialogues, confronts distrust, puts shifting relationships on equal ground, and brings what's important to the forefront of our lives.

Looking back on my choice to be silent in the face of tragedy, to pretend, to feign strength, I understand something significant, even though I had to learn it the hard way. The lie behind silence is that God is not good or able to heal. It's a distorted self-confidence that tries to manage pain on its own instead of trusting that there is something beyond, Someone who is far greater than the crushing weight we often try to shoulder on our own.

"Smiling depression" is what Edward T. Welch calls this kind of pretending in his book *Depression: Looking Up from the Stubborn Darkness*.[1] I remember reading these words shortly after my father died and realizing that it described both me and him. I had deceived myself into believing that I could smile my way through the onset of a deadly sort of depression, while he believed that smiling could avoid the truth of his.

I know that a majority of this world doesn't believe a capital-H Healer even exists. And I often wonder, how do they cope? The woman whose body has been exploited. The child who has been broken. The man who has become an outcast. Don't they need to know that there is One who has suffered with them, for them?

Isn't a healer ultimately one who understands pain?

THE REALITY OF POSITIVITY

So many people wanted to know how a man like my father—someone filled with "joy"—could have ended his own life. He had spent so much of his time helping and encouraging people who were less capable than he. He preached the same lesson to me over and over again. "Lynne," he would say later on in life, a serious but meaningful half-smile on his face, "You just have to be positive."

Positive?

I had no answer to the throngs of confused people unable to connect my father's "joy" with his death. It was hard to accept, but the real lesson—the dreadful truth—was that he didn't know any other way to make himself believe his pain wasn't real. He was a stoic. He wished deep secrets, unbearable pains, and bleeding wounds into nonexistence. Little did he know that they would only coalesce against him on that Last Day.

Look around and remember this: my father was, by far, not the only one.

DIFFERENT TYPES OF DISHONESTY

Healing demands honesty.

That means a lot of things, especially in the midst of pain. Sometimes honesty means being authentic to other people about how you feel. Sometimes it means not lying to yourself about whatever internal war your emotions are fighting. Sometimes it means learning that trying to escape pain is never a way to cope with it. Different circumstances demand different kinds of honesty.

For me, honesty meant that stoicism was not an option. Being afraid of the roiling, visceral output of emotion that was so real inside me was sickness itself. Being encouraged to stay that way by someone who I should have been able to trust was a dangerous prescription. I remember that encounter with frustration and anger, but I also remember that many people aren't aware of the Healer's presence.

They don't realize that silence leads to suffering just as deceit leads to death. Max Lucado shares the following story in *Just like Jesus*.

Many years ago, a man conned his way into the orchestra of the emperor of China although he could not play a note. Whenever the group practiced or performed, he would hold his flute against his lips, pretending to play but not making a sound. He received a modest salary and enjoyed a comfortable living. Then one day the emperor requested a solo from each musician. The flouter got nervous. There wasn't enough time to learn the instrument. He pretended to be sick, but the royal physician wasn't fooled. On the day of his performance, the impostor took poison and killed himself. The explanation of his suicide led to a phrase that found its way into the English language: "He refused to face the music."[2]

The world isn't fooled by deception. We can only pretend for as long as we force ourselves and believe the lie that deception promotes. It's common for lies to go unnoticed, hidden just long enough to be forgotten. It's more common for them to fester until they explode, ugly and destructive, each its own kind of monster. No amount of stoicism can truly counteract an untruth.

Another way people are dishonest in the face of pain is what I'm going to call, "people-pleasing."

People-pleasing is a way to escape the rejection and verbal attack that may accompany pain. It allows you to hide behind pleasantries and yeses. It's easier to deal with the hardships that accompany conflict if you just make people happy.

Happiness is easy to fake but hard to get. I often think of that visitor who admonished me to "get a hold of myself." What really mattered in that moment? That I get it together because she thought I should or because I *needed* it? The fact was, I needed to be honest about who I was in that moment, which was broken, sore, and devastated.

Muffling grief by trying to make other people happy is as unhealthy as it is unnecessary. But I want to consider its devastating effects.

Imagine the people-pleaser as a marionette. It dangles sloppily until it's presented with an audience. Then it dances. It's an uneven, unrealistic dance, driven by the subtleties of pent-up pain, toxic emotions, and minced words. All of this is controlled by a horrible master—anger. Anger makes us dance for others. It makes us dance until we can't any longer. It makes us dance to the tune of depression, anxiety, and suppressed rage.

It's a twisted show and one that's avoidable.

Escape is one other way that people are dishonest with themselves in the face of pain.

Pain is easily and quickly dealt with by unconsciousness. That's why so many people turn to drugs and alcohol. It's a quick and simple way out of misery. Lose your bearings on the world by prohibiting your mind from thinking about it, and the problem's solved–for a little while.

Maybe substances aren't as attractive as other types of self-harm. People often turn to cutting, bleeding themselves out like a sacrifice before pain's altar. But, like substances, one cut always demands another. Short of self-destruction, you can't bleed your way to oblivion.

Then there's sexual escape. A virtual amusement park of sexual perversion is available to anyone who wants it. Pornography is the opiate of many who just don't want to remember the hurt. But a fantasy is only temporary. You can build castles in the sky, but they crumble and leave you and your pain in the darkness together.

These are just a handful of ways that humans avoid pain. As long as we've experienced pain, we've invented a countless number of ways to run away from reality, to dull the excruciating feeling. But the world has also learned that true healing isn't easy. It is not quick. It is not simple. It's not fun. It's not pleasant. But the consequences of ignoring it are far, far worse.

Victims of those consequences walk among us today. Each one is a living grave filled with self-neglect, resentment, depression, passive-aggressive behaviors, and, ultimately, a joyless existence.

What we desperately want to be the cure is actually the curse.

A TIME TO WEEP, A TIME TO LAUGH

But that's not the end of the story.

Healing begins when we stop and consider the

consequences of silenced pain. Suppressed anger will destroy relationships, and escape will slowly drain you of your humanity. Stoicism is a ticking bomb. So what other options are there?

In Ecclesiastes 3:1, Solomon said, "There is an appointed time for everything. And there is a time for every event under heaven." He goes on to illustrate his point by talking about the dichotomies that everyday life is often made of.

This is no lie. God Himself has ordained circumstances. Not randomly but with purpose. There is, says Solomon, "A time to weep and a time to laugh; a time to mourn and a time to dance" (Ecclesiastes 3:4). These are not contradictions. They are appointed realities of life that exist to grow, change, and renew us.

In order to understand this kind of wisdom, we have to look at both sides of the dichotomy. Solomon reminds us of two important things.

1. We have to treat each moment accordingly. "Weeping" (to use the writer's term for sadness or pain) is not "laughing," and if we fool ourselves into thinking it is, we'll be hopelessly confused.

2. Pain is temporary. Part of healing is remembering what's on the other side. What is torn down can be rebuilt, just as what is torn will be whole again. Just like the pain,

joy is appointed.

If you and I choose to see our pain as though it were a disease to be diagnosed and treated rather than appointed, we risk the symptoms of hopelessness. Pain is not a pathological ailment. It's one of the heart's ultimate expressions of humanity.

Look at it like this. The heart has a story that it needs to share. Stories remind us that pain and joy have their appropriate places. When we tell the whole story just as it is—or allow it to be told—healing begins.

My story needed to be told in the moments after my father's death when I was broken, completely languishing, crying out and weeping. It was the only way that I began to understand what was happening to me. The more I understood who I was, what had happened, and what was going to happen, the stronger I became.

It was a strange but beautiful kind of wisdom.

SURRENDER

Everything I've said in this chapter pales in comparison to this final truth.

What's on trial through suffering is not whether or not healing is possible but *where* our healing comes from. When we exhaust all of our own fallible weapons to combat pain, we must look to the infinite Hope and an infallible Healer.

Jesus, the One of whom it says in Isaiah 61:1–3, "He has sent me to bind up the brokenhearted . . . to comfort all who mourn . . . giving them a garland instead of ashes, the oil of gladness instead of mourning." He is that healer.

If Jesus promoted one thing, it was the truth, a quality that He embodied. If living balanced means that we must live close to the truth, it also means that we must live close to Christ.

Honesty connects us to faith. So much of what distracts us from reality is too much trust in ourselves or in others. God has given us intellect, intuition, and good advice to follow. But more importantly, He gave us Jesus.

A lot of our self-deceptions are cloaked in fear of what others will think of us. We don't want to look abnormal, so we shield ourselves with lies.

But God is too good to let us save ourselves. His goodness is not diminished because I feel pain or because I choose to run away from it. He is so good that our pain can be a path to understand and embrace His goodness. This kind of honesty is the most authentic. If you can fall on your knees before the One who made you and loves you, letting your anguish thrust you into His presence, you can also be healed.

Balance is surrender to the Healer.

ANGUISH IS OKAY

I don't want to sugarcoat it. Getting out of bed wasn't easy after my father died. Even in the days when I learned to be honest and draw closer to God, I still struggled to greet the morning with hope. Sometimes I still do.

I also understood that healing was a process.

Slowly, carefully, I allowed myself to weep when I needed to weep and to be strong when I needed to be strong. That sounds simple, but it wasn't always. Knowing the truth and acting on it are two different things.

But I acted on it, even when I had to force myself.

Most of all, it was an encouragement to me to remember the truth of what Christ Himself did *already* to help me cope. "He was pierced through for our transgressions, He was crushed for our iniquities," it says in Isaiah 53:5. And I believed it.

Maybe it's unconventional, but I want to tell you that it's okay to cry, to be in anguish, to lament. Evil exists, and it has touched our lives. That doesn't mean we have to let it consume us. If we are hurt by it, we don't have to hide it. But we do have to answer it.

I began this chapter with a quote that I believe encapsulates everything I'm hoping for those who are still reeling from the aftershocks of pain.

"Your joy is your sorrow unmasked."

Herein are two wonderful truths that spell the beginning of a hope-filled life.

First, you don't have to wear a mask.

Second, your sorrow is *going* to turn into joy.

If you believe this, healing isn't far away.

Living balanced means that we must live close to the truth—it means that we must live close to Christ, our healer.

Chapter 4

Identity Thieves

Your real, new self will not come as long as you are looking for it. It will come when you are looking for Him.
C. S. Lewis

A THIEF IN THE NIGHT

I remember nights like this one all too vividly.

With everyone else in the house asleep, I would make a slow and careful journey to the coat closet. After years of practice, I knew the creaks in the floor by heart and how to avoid them. I knew when the door hinges would groan. I knew how to time every movement just right. No one could suspect what they didn't know was there.

When I made it to the closet, I'd reach through the darkness. I knew where everything was, even though I was blind. I found the gap, peeled back the cardboard, got what I had come for, and continued on my mission.

To the kitchen, specifically the sink. I was practiced enough to know that if I was careful, the sound of liquid pouring down the drain wouldn't force up air with a popping sound if I poured slowly. The downside of pouring slowly was the awful stench of the stuff. *How can people drink this?* I'd wonder as I ran a tiny stream of water down to clear the air and cover my tracks even further. The smell faded to be replaced with that ounce of hope I was looking for.

I worked backward to bed and slept another victorious night.

One more empty beer bottle. Twelve-year-old me was confident she was part of a great work.

I could not have been more wrong.

SUICIDE SURVIVOR?

In 2007 I was looking for answers and being proactive about the healing process. I wanted to practice honesty in community—something that was not easy to come by. Being with others whose lives had been tilted by suicide seemed like a good way to reach out and understand myself more at the same time.

So I signed up for a "Suicide Walk" in my hometown. There I would gather with other victims, parents, brothers and sisters, children like me, friends, all walking to identify their grief and mourn the lost.

Or so I thought.

Even before the walk started, I felt unsettled. The

organizers shuffled in and out of the crowd of participants, handing out colored bead necklaces.

"What are these for?" I asked. This wasn't Mardi Gras. This was serious.

"The colors represent your relationship to the person who died," they told me. "Your color is gold because you lost a parent." Frustrated, I wore the faux jewelry and walked.

But I couldn't shake the discomfort. "I feel empty and this stupid necklace isn't helping. I've got a scar on my heart, and they expect me to navigate my pain with plastic beads?"

As I walked, I thought about what the event called us: "Suicide Survivors."

I was a suicide survivor, wasn't I? I looked around me. We were all suicide survivors. But then I saw something that horrified me.

I walked quicker. I wanted this to be over. It was all wrong. I walked with the herd until I couldn't stand it anymore, and I turned around and walked away. I couldn't look at those faces anymore, and I certainly couldn't be one of them.

This wasn't healing. This was a bunch of pain-filled individuals huddling together under the banner of their hurt.

I was many things on that day, but Suicide Survivor

wasn't one of them. I knew then and there that if healing, grace, and honesty were going to be a real part of my story, there had to be more to my life than the thing that had tilted it beyond recognition.

IDENTITY CRISIS

What do you think when you hear the words "identity crisis"? It's about someone losing touch with who they really are, right? Everyone's got to have a disaster concerning acceptance, value, purpose, or image at some point in their life, don't they?

It's true, humans are often obsessed with their identity. What we call a "crisis" is often a person who's become very worried about how he or she is perceived. The older we get, the more we think ourselves experts in the idea of who we are, and we get scared or angry when that idea falls apart or goes awry.

We are fragile enough to be broken by an identity crisis, and that's frightening.

We live in a world where almost no identity is safe. Whether it's a person or a new idea or a possession or a life event, our self-perception and our ideal self can be smashed to bits in moments.

Is it surprising, then, that when you build your ideal self

around something unstable, you too will feel and be unstable?

That, I think, is what scared me so much at the Suicide Walk. I looked around and saw people who were embracing an identity of brokenness, leaving emotional health and healing by the wayside.

There's nothing new about this phenomenon. It happens to many people. But that doesn't make it any more tolerable or realistic. In fact, I chose early on to think of identity through a simple metaphorical idea.

Identity—real, genuine personhood—lives inside all of us. But we live in a tilted world, and when crises of all types strike, our identities are stolen. We are robbed. And where authenticity once dwelt is now replaced with fear, pain, suppression, doubt, abuse, self-sufficiency, and a host of other things that are the furthest thing imaginable from the real you. I call these "identity thieves," and I've seen my fair share of them in both myself and others who lead lives thrown out of balance by pain.

NOT ENOUGH

Those nights when I would sneak from my bedroom to the place where my father kept his alcohol to the sink where I tried to wash it all away forever—those nights were my first lessons in identity.

My father was an alcoholic. For reasons that are never simple to explain, he made a decision to let drink define him. For reasons that are very *easy* to explain, I adopted the identity of his savior. Someone had to rescue him from the beast he was becoming, and if no one else was brave enough just to pour that stuff down the drain, I would have to do it myself. I was trying to give his life back to him, to save it and, perhaps, my own.

Ultimately, it wasn't the alcohol that turned my dad into what he became. It was something else, something I've never been able to put my finger on. Was it "not good enough"? Was it "not successful enough"? Perhaps "not rich or smart enough"? Or, maybe, it was simply "not *enough*."

And while he grasped at emptiness, I pushed the emptiness away. I didn't want my identity to be "child of an alcoholic" just as much as I wanted to redefine my father as "sober and dedicated dad." These were well intentioned, but both of us, though I think we desired the right thing, were out of touch with ourselves.

You've probably already assumed this, but it was a

time of immense pain for me. My father's alcoholism was more than just an addiction; it was a monster puppeteer, dangling our whole family by seemingly unbreakable strings.

That's the simple but horrific power of an identity thief.

A LESSON FROM THE SNEETCHES

This is weighty stuff, I know. So it's ironic I find one of the best illustrations of stolen identities from the work of a man who made a career out of delighting people.

Dr. Seuss's *The Sneetches* always intrigued me. It's a story about sneetches, which are creatures living on a beach where everything is okay, except that one group of these quirky things—the ones with stars on their bellies—disdains the other. It's a simple tale that handles everything from segregation (the separation of the two externally differentiated groups) to the flux of status symbols, as when the sneetches alter their bodies over and over again in an attempt to be supremely special. After a sneaky salesman named McBean tries to make a profit on the belly-star market with his star-on, star-off machines, a hectic race to be "the best" commences. Midway through the story, the sneetches are utterly confused, to say the least.[1]

I think we're like sneetches. Our "stars" are supremely important to us. We go back and forth donning careers, degrees, awards, friendships, athletic achievements. Even things like sporting events, cars, hobbies, projects, clothes, and nice homes vie for significance in our lives.

Like the sneetches, I think we take on and put off our stars, pretending from one moment to the next that we are something other than our true selves. Like any practice based in untruth, this is a self-defeating habit. No matter how bad our true identities are, discarding them for the sake of pretending is always harmful. Lies always attack the people who tell them.

IDENTITY THIEVES

We desire love. We thirst for acceptance. And we want these cravings to be noticed and affirmed. We grasp for control as we cling to the belief that its presence will ensure a future filled with safety and security. The chatter of our lives crescendos with each passing day. We demand purpose and meaning as part of our identity, as if its fulfillment is the way in which our life procreates. As our appetite to understand who we are increases, so do our methods to find nourishment. We find ourselves nursing anything that promises it can satisfy our deepest longings. Endlessly, we root. Like a newborn, we latch onto anything we believe will pour forth life-giving nourishment, something to fulfill our visceral appetites and create an identity our soul considers satisfying.

But, do we ever stop to question what it is we long for? Do we ever consider whether what is pouring into us nourishes or depletes? Not always. Sometimes we simply continue to feed on fake things, things that are ultimately unsatisfying.

I call people, beliefs, circumstances, or practices that we identify with that distort the truth of who we are "identity thieves." These are like mirrors we preen ourselves in, pretending we're better than we actually are. We become the offspring of their lies, because they have fed our appetites. Appetites that have created strong desires that have led to lives grasping for anything selling fulfillment. Like McBean's star-on, star-off machine, we never stop to question these thieves. We simply buy the lie and sell our souls.

So many of us are drifting further away from ourselves because of these lies, lost and frightened by the core of who we are and what we were created to be. In our drifting, people, careers, self-help books and retreats, activities and busyness, sporting events and teams, sickness, children and families—and even our pain and dysfunction—become our anchors. We sprint, arms open and ready to embrace anything that will tame the restlessness from not knowing who we are. All of these have purpose in growing us. However, they are poor substitutes for defining us. In the end, we are robbed of our identities.

LOOKING FOR SOLUTIONS

We're also robbed of a sense of destination. How are we supposed to get to healing if we're so addicted to a made-up idea of ourselves?

Regaining balance requires letting go. When we remove our grip on the temporary, we are restored because we have surrendered to the only One who can hold us up. "Come to Me, all who are weary and heavy-laden," He promises, "and I will give you rest" (Matthew 11:28). A rest from striving from the slave masters selling their idols of identity, a rest from the thieves that distort and ultimately wound through empty promises, and a rest from ourselves. Rest. Sweet rest.

When we rest, we're giving ourselves to the rightful owner of our destinies—Jesus Christ. It is not our experiences, our flaws, careers or accomplishments, friends, families, acquaintances, pursuits, degrees, beliefs, or our busyness that define us. He alone is the identity-maker.

I belonged to God, and He alone would determine what needed fixing in my life and how He was going to accomplish His magnum opus in me. I was not a suicide survivor or an adult child of an alcoholic. We are wise to consider our flaws in light of good counsel, but we should never accept as our image the reflection through a fallen man or woman, event, or man-made institutions or rules. The mirror of man is cracked, and so then is the image it reflects. Man's broken reflection, institutions, and social norms and theories of who we are is always changing and in flux, and this produces an emotional and mental instability that will always keep life off balance.

Changing this unbalanced lifestyle requires risk and honesty. Often we are not willing to risk change, because change brings unfamiliar roles and responsibilities. Depending on a lie is easier than living independent from truth. Truth is hard, because it requires daily rehearsing of new material. But lies are exhausting.

We have a lot of confidence in our own solutions. Like the sneetches, we insanely ramp up our efforts using the same solutions, believing that our rest is found in grinding harder and spending more of ourselves. We have believed the modern day incantation "no pain, no gain." Refusing to settle, we willingly enslave ourselves to a system built on the foundation of failure. Because we focus on the technique of our effort, we become blinded to the need to evaluate the outcome.

Did it really matter if I poured one bottle of beer down the drain or ten? Would drinking ten beers have been a better resolution than drinking one? What I did not know then but do now, is that doing nothing was really the solution. Why? Because I was a child of the King. He could take care of my dad. He didn't need me. I could rest in His creative solutions. The only impact my efforts had was to place my trust in the wrong object and system of beliefs and rules. I became my own solution and source of sorrow.

I AM

Strength is surrender. Surrender your identity and hope to the One who says "[you] are fearfully and wonderfully made. Wonderful are [My] works" (Psalm 139:14). We have a God who stamps us as approved (Genesis 1:31). We are His creation, and each day of our life has been ordained in advance (Psalm 139:16). Working harder does not reveal our identity. Working harder only increases our guilt over our failures and pushes us even harder to take on more doing in hopes of finding an increase in value to our self-worth.

Surrender is active and courageous. It requires a daily, personal decision to relinquish the old systems we use to define ourselves: people, pain, circumstances, society, and old beliefs. The choice to choose God, our Creator, as our source of identity frees us from the cycle of insanity. When God spoke to Moses and instructed him to go to His chosen people, the Israelites, and prepare them for their deliverance from oppression, Moses inquired who he was to say sent him. God's reply was simple: "I AM." The great God of heaven, creator and sustainer of the earth, wanted to be known as the great "I AM." No credentials required. Simply, "I AM."

The answer God provided resonated with these people, because they understood the identity of the One who spoke "I AM." God, the great "I AM," was their deliverer throughout their turbulent, often painful history. His name was both His reputation and His identity. His purpose was to help the Israelites walk with confidence in who He was and not who their captors were at the time, the Egyptians. They were enslaved, but they were not slaves. They were "persecuted, but not forsaken; struck down, but not destroyed" (2 Corinthians 4:9). God was on the move, and He needed to remind them of their true identity: chosen, loved, and purposed.

God, this great "I AM," wants us to remember our identity in His promises, His character, and His reputation. The great "I AM" wants to set us free and invites us to rest in the identity He has ordained for us since the beginning of time. (See Psalm 139.)

The "I AM" holds an intact mirror up to us, and if we still our souls long enough, we can behold our true identity. The problem we face, however, is that we believe this mirror is a moving object subject to change as our circumstances change.

But we are the ones moving. We move like the thief in an attempt to not get caught. We fear stillness. We fear the moment stillness allows us to look into the mirror and surrender to truth. We do not want to see the pain that time and events and people have inflicted. We become our own identity thieves when we refuse to surrender.

HE WALKS WITH ME

The Healer, the great "I AM," however, does not wish for us to focus on the pain but the solution to the pain. The truth of who we are in Him. The evidence of this truth repeats itself throughout Scripture.

I am loved: "I have loved you with an everlasting love; Therefore I have drawn you with lovingkindness." (Jeremiah 31:3)

I am heard: "I love the Lord, because He hears my voice and my supplications [my earnest pleas and cries] . . . He has inclined His ear to me." (Psalm 116:1)

I am healed: "He heals the brokenhearted and binds up their wounds." (Psalm 147:3)

I am forgiven: "[Christ] who pardons [forgives] all your iniquities [sins]." (Psalm 103:3)

I am seen: "You are a God who sees." (Genesis 16:13)

I am gifted and talented: "God's gifts [talents] are handed out everywhere [to everyone]. (1 Corinthians 12:7 The Message)

"Since we have gifts [talents] . . . each of us is to exercise [use] them." (Romans 12:6)

"For the gifts and the calling [purpose] of God are irrevocable." (Romans 11:29)

I am prayed for: See John 17.

I am delivered: "Deliver [me] from evil. For Yours is the kingdom and the power." (Matthew 6:13)

I am satisfied and renewed: "[He] who satisfies your years with good things, so that your youth is renewed like the eagle." (Psalm 103:5)

I am protected: "He will cover you with His pinions [arms], and under His wings [arms] you may seek refuge [safety]; His faithfulness is a shield and bulwark [a defensive wall]." (Psalm 91:4)

I am bestowed peace: "Peace I leave with you . . . Do not let your heart be troubled, nor let it be fearful." (John 14:27)

I am comforted: "who comforts us in all our affliction [troubles]." (2 Corinthians 1:4)

I am strong when I am weak: "My grace is sufficient [enough] for you, for power is perfected in weakness." (2 Corinthians 12:9)

I am free: "He [Christ] ... proclaim[s] liberty to captives and freedom to prisoners." (Isaiah 61:1)

I am changed: "If anyone is in Christ, he [or she] is a new creature [person]; the old things [the old ways have] passed away; behold, new things [a new way of living and doing] have come." (2 Corinthians 5:17)

When our identity is anchored in Christ, we, like the lyrist to the song "Sheltered in the Arms of God," can sing
So let the storms rage high,
The dark clouds rise,

> *They don't worry me;*
> *For I'm sheltered safe within the arms of God.*
> *He walks with me,*
> *And naught of earth shall harm me,*
> *For I'm sheltered in the arms of God.*[2]

God is our shelter, our safe haven, our rock. He is our identity.

You are who God says you are and not what your feelings, circumstances, or experiences try to establish. Externals do not have the power to write your story. You choose your response. Ignore the shifting sands of your own weaknesses, pains, failures, and doubts. Build your identity on Christ, the eternal, solid Rock.

Rest in Him, and you will stand balanced. Look for Him and find yourself.

Living balanced requires letting go of the broken mirrors of man we preen in front of for the sake of defining who we are.

Chapter 5

Compassion's Counterweight

The individual is capable of both great compassion and great indifference. He has it within his means to nourish the former and outgrow the latter.

Norman Cousins

UNEXPECTED KINDNESS

I lay on the couch. I cannot possibly get to the bathroom one more time. Limp with exhaustion, I search for a solution to my body's constant demand to emit the contents of my stomach. I scan the room, spot my hope–the item that will allow me to be both stationary and sick–my mother's well-worn, well-used roasting pot. It's deep and able to hold the contents of my stomach, which refuses to comply with my desire for immediate healing.

In my weakness, I arrange for the pot to rest on a towel placed near my head on the floor. Now I can conserve my energy and simply lift my head from our couch to empty the contents of my stomach. What typically serves nourishment will now receive back from me the nourishment my body is so violently rejecting. Quietly the hours pass as I lay silently on my makeshift hospital bed.

My dad is home. I hear him open the back door, but I don't care about his lack of relationship with me. I'm too weak. I look up, and he's coming toward me. My dry mouth begins to salivate as I don't know what response to expect from him. His eyes look from me to the floor, where I've arranged my makeshift emesis basin. I'm frightened. My mind has created a variety of unkind responses to expect from this man who harshly responds to life.

His voice is uncharacteristically tender and his body movements gentle. His delicate approach softens the emotional tension I feel. Lovingly, he removes the pot and replaces it with a lined container. The softness in his voice removes the guilt I feel of mistakenly choosing the wrong object to contain my vomit. "Here, honey, let's use something else," are his only words. They're enough to calm me and erase my fear. When he's done, he walks away. I don't hear or see him for the remainder of the day.

In time, my body heals. What remains is not the memory of my misery that summer day but the compassion my father granted me in my suffering. His compassionate act was unfamiliar to me, but I received it like a thirsty dog parched from the heat of summer. His gesture of compassion begins to soften the hard places my heart had been protecting due to years of stern silence between a father and a daughter.

FEARLESS LOVE

Compassion heals because its intent is to connect to the heart of the suffering and misfortune that can plague people's lives. Compassion prepares the way for Christ, the Healer, to heal. Compassion reaches out to connect with its target, but it isn't in the reaching that healing takes place. Compassion touches, and it's in this touch where hope is ignited and healing germinates and exerts its curative powers.

Jesus leaves a powerful example of the power of compassion's healing touch in Matthew 8:1–3. In this account of healing, Jesus is approached by a leper. A man lawfully condemned as unclean, an outcast from society. The leper kneels before Him and states, "Lord, if You are willing, You can make me clean." Jesus, full of compassion, "reached out His hand and touched" him. Then Jesus says, "I'm willing. Be clean."

Jesus was willing to reach and touch society's most disdained citizen. Compassion compelled Him to reach and touch.

I imagine his family and friends may have experienced deep emotional pain for this leper in his physical suffering and mental and emotional anguish. But their feelings couldn't transform his condition, nor could they alter his position in society. What transformed him was compassion's willingness to both reach and touch—a willingness that went against societal fear.

Fear is compassion's nemesis. Fear draws back from the sick, the hopeless, the misunderstood. Instead of being compassionate, fear judges. It's self-preserving, because the one withholding the touch of compassion fears the smear of pain rubbing off onto himself.

I know. I recall the moment when fear withheld the much-needed and hoped for arm of compassion.

THE VOLUNTEER

"That is the most selfish act a person can do!"

"Why would anyone do that to their family?"

"How cruel!"

"Well, life is for the living."

Spoken with conviction and indignation, many people thought they were releasing me of any guilt I shouldered from my father's suicide. But each declaration became an assault against an imperfect man whom I called "Dad." What they didn't understand or seek to know was that my father's final act did not define his sixty-seven years of life.

Whether it began that day on the couch or years later, I

don't know. But what I observed was that sometime in his life, compassion changed him. Compassion had softened a tormented man who'd suffered years of mental anguish and a past riddled with secrets he chose to keep encrypted in his psyche. Compassion had done for him what it was doing for me: bring the outcast back into the circle of God's healing presence.

My dad shared his compassion through a variety of volunteer opportunities. Tirelessly he transported children to the Shriner's hospital. There, these children would find hope and healing through a myriad of medical professionals and support staff. He marched in endless parades to raise money for the work of this benevolent organization.

While volunteering at the hospital, he took great joy in extending words of kindness and encouragement to staff, visitors, and patients. He made room in his heart for people and supplied generous amounts of forgiveness to those whose lives had been bulleted by careless acts of sin. He understood the need to forgive, because he himself had been granted such mercy for his poor judgments and missteps. In his advancing years, my dad somehow conveyed the notion, "I understand. I've been there too." Because compassion had softened him, he was able to become a vehicle through which others would begin their journey into healing.

His transformation from harsh to gentle became my catalyst to understanding the beauty, gift, and transforming power of compassion.

What I couldn't understand is how those whose harsh and critical responses to his final decision could heal my broken heart. It was their comments that threw me off balance, not my dad's casket. What I needed was for those passing judgment to extend compassion and not use their fear—veiled in compassion—as a shield to blunt my expression of pain.

Jesus used both words and touch to remove the shame of the leper's pain and disgrace. I, too, needed people to bless my dad's memory with kind words that would touch my soul and ignite the torch of healing. Compassion. This is what I longed for, both for me and my father.

COUNTERWEIGHT

Compassion is the counterweight to a life tilt. It balances the load between pain, suffering, hope, and healing. It keeps the sufferer from emotionally and mentally crashing into the abyss of their dark experience of pain and sorrow. It allows them to believe that tomorrow holds bright, life-giving color and that not all of life is washed in hopeless black and grey. Compassion is God's rainbow of hope and His balancing rod for restoration.

When you extend compassion, it allows you to look beyond the flaws and brokenness of the one it touches. It looks past soiled lives, hostile emotions, fear and uncertainty, confusion, misunderstanding, and the wounded years that sin has stolen from humanity. It chooses to overlook an offense, because it makes room for sin. In fact, compassion allows sin to present itself out front—safely—and be confronted with the love and forgiveness required for healing to mend what sin has broken. With compassion, we convey that acceptance isn't dependent upon perfection but on the selfless motive of the one sharing in the suffering and extending comfort.

Many days I was confronted with the sting of someone's criticism. I'm not sure what their criticism was protecting them from. I believe their critical daggers were really reflections of what lay hidden in the depth of their hearts. When you follow the path of criticism, you often discover people are trying to protect others from seeing their own imperfect lives.

Is it possible that people who lie criticize liars, that a cheat is critical of a cheater, or that a selfish person points the finger and cries out "selfish, selfish" to a suicide victim? Can personal sin or insecurity be varnished over by criticism directed at another's transgression? To this I say, yes.

Healing and balance come when we use compassion to confront offense, pain, sorrow, and misunderstanding. The reason compassion heals is because it's not afraid to touch the unclean, the social leper society invented. It reaches through the dark places that criticism barricades. It brings people back into the circle of belongingness and into the light of Christ's transformative and powerful touch.

THE FORGIVING SIDE OF COMPASSION

Part of compassion's restorative nature is through extending forgiveness. Forgiveness restores balance when it's willingly extended to those who are living on the periphery of your life tilt that have misunderstood or misjudged the elements within your life journey.

Forgiveness is both a gift to you and to those whose sin is layered by a false knowledge of what is right and true about your life situation or circumstance. Forgiveness releases the offender by reminding the offended that the cause of social leprosy isn't the focus—the Healer is.

Many times I reminded myself that I didn't owe anyone an explanation of who my father was or even feign to offer a narrative for his choice. I released my offenders by seeing the pain and confusion of their well-intended attempts to render healing through misguided words. What I wasn't sure of was whether or not their offensive remarks were a way to reduce their discomfort that my pain had created or to offer me assurance that I was without guilt in my dad's decision. In the end, it didn't matter. What was important wasn't who or what had offended but what I was going to do with the offense and the offender.

Forgiveness gives up the right to blame others. It provides balance as it places the one forgiving back in control of their life. Unforgiveness is me handcuffing myself to my offender. Once I place the handcuffs on, I take the offender with me everywhere I go—emotionally, mentally, spiritually, and sometimes physically. The declining health of the offended provides the evidence.

At first it's easy to take our offender with us, but as time progresses, our level of personal and emotional fatigue increases. We become weary and easily angered. We wait and wait for the offender to see how embattled we are. We want them to recognize our emotional and psychological pain. *Surely they will see and come to know how burdensome my load is*, we surmise.

But what we the offended forget is that we've personally swallowed the toxic dose of an offense, believing the offender will suffocate under his or her guilt and beg forgiveness. The reality is that we, the offended, are the one suffocating from carrying around the offender and their offense every moment of our life. We're the one off balance, not them. The simple truth is that we cuffed them to us and only the offended holds the key that unlocks the cuffs and sets both us and them free.

Living with compassion grows us into people who reflect the beauty and grace of God's character, as it reminds us of the flaws and foibles we have been forgiven. It unites us to our offender as we stand bare before God, reminded that, in His love, He covered our shame with His compassion.

Our eyes have been opened, and we see a world that stands in need of healing and a Healer. It's God's way of reminding us of what we have been given and entrusted with, and that it's our duty and loving obligation to share in His gifts.[1] Our worth isn't based on how good or perfect we are but on God's gift of perfect love.

Our lives can at times resemble wrecked trains, derailed, emotional debris strewn everywhere. Compassion is willing to risk time and repair the damage of life's unexpected spills. Compassion returns balance because we see Him, not ourselves, and we see others *through* Him.

YOU ARE NOT ALONE

There's a warmth to the radiant glow of compassion,

because it reminds us we are not alone. When my husband and I purchased our second home, we weren't prepared for life on a rural county road. We moved in May of 1997 and enjoyed the beauty and warmth of that summer. Having never lived without the protection of a community, we soon learned the importance of people sharing in hardships.

Our first winter, we lost power for three days. With no heat, water, generator, or source to warm food, we endured bone-chilling temperatures. Roads were closed, and so was our customary way of living. We lit slender dining candles in hope of having light and staying warm. I brought my youngest daughter into my bed, and together we conserved energy under layers of clothing and bedding.

My oldest daughter was with my mother, who also lived in the country and was without power. At the age of seven, my daughter was distraught over not being able to return home to the reassuring arms of her mother. To her advantage, my mother had a gas-powered stove.

After three days of these harsh events, my neighbor, several doors down, had his power restored. He and his wife brought us into their home, fed us, and provided the warmth and basic necessities we so desperately craved. Upon hearing of the plight of my oldest daughter, my neighbor offered to hook the plow to the front end of his truck and attempt a rescue mission to bring my daughter home.

Ed understood my heart need and selflessly reached out to help. Not willing to allow him to risk his life on my behalf, I joined him on the mission. Together, we bare-knuckled it across roads stretched with layers of snow and ice. What normally would have been a fifteen-minute drive took over an hour.

I will never forget the little girl, arms stretched out, so delighted to see her mother. My arrival and presence became the soul assuring and warmth my daughter needed to calm her frightful soul. My presence was my love reaching out through compassion.

I, too, felt the warmth of Ed and his wife, Melanie, as they reached out and allowed compassion to lead their decision to provide humanity's basic need—love. Their compassion warmed me to the core and blessed me by reminding me I was not alone.

When we build walls around our hearts and don't allow the tendrils of compassion to enter or exit, our spirit man becomes impoverished. We become prisoners of our own painful existence. Compassion tears down those walls and provides the nourishment that love provides. We must be willing to both extend and receive compassion.

Compassion is a counterweight, because it makes us less vindictive toward others. It allows us to look tenderly into another's eyes and discover what causes their pain. Our pain lessens when we refuse, under any condition, to inflict more pain or judgment or to withhold mercy and grace from any person.

One of the greatest fruits to grow from compassion is encouragement. Encouragement fortifies us as it becomes the fuel to take the next painful step in the hard places of life. It helps us accept our failures as lessons toward success. Encouragement kills the weeds of doubt and hatred as it becomes the vision necessary to see the other person as they are: fragile, imperfect, vulnerable, and spiritually in need of ongoing growth and change.

BOUNDLESS, ENDLESS

I vividly remember reading an article on suicide written by a Catholic priest. His words penetrated my heart with encouragement when he reminded his readers that God's compassion and grace could enter places ours could not. It was then that I could release my uncertainty of my dad's journey into the afterlife. I now envisioned a God whose compassion could reach through to a man who'd been encrypted by concrete and marble.

It was the first time I believed with certainty that death could not stop the work of compassion. I could see a God whose love could not be barricaded by a gun. I could only imagine that God's compassion tenderly reached into the casket my dad's body had been laid in and that God Himself was now the only One who could touch and heal a tormented soul. My dad had accepted the work of Christ in his life, and now the cross continued its work in him.

Compassion has no boundaries and is endless.

Lamentations 3:22–23 reminds us that "The Lord's lovingkindness indeed never cease, for His compassions never fail. They are new every morning; great is Your faithfulness."

Florence Littauer writes, "So often we think that to be encouragers we have to produce great words of wisdom when, in fact, a few simple syllables of sympathy and an arm around the shoulder can often provide much needed comfort."[2]

I imagined my dad resting with the arms of Jesus around him, providing the comfort he so longed for. In this belief, I could feel Christ's arms around me, providing the comfort a daughter so desperately longed for from a Father.

Compassion had changed me. That is what compassion does. It allowed me to take my hands off the offense that criticism had created and walk unencumbered. I was free now to love unhindered.

We have a choice of what we will nourish in our lives.

I choose to nourish the seed of compassion that began with a simple act of kindness so many years ago, when a father became a dad. Balance requires compassion and not criticism. Choose balance. Live in compassion.

Living balanced requires compassion, given and received, and not criticism to fill our thinking and our lives.

Chapter 6

Lingering

Sometimes it's worth lingering on the journey for a while before getting to the destination.
Richelle Mead

A CLUMSY DANCE

I like to dance, but I don't know how. It's better to smile and exit the dance floor than to experience the humiliation of staying and allowing the ability to be nurtured with time and experience. My dad's visits always felt like this clumsy dance.

Growing up, I knew not to get too comfortable when we visited friends and relatives. Barely warmed up, after our social greetings and platitudes, it would be time to gear up and exit. Oftentimes it appeared to take more time to don shoes on and off than it took to visit with the hosts.

When I was married, my father's visits to my home were no different. I could sense his readiness to bolt the moment he entered the threshold. I never understood his restlessness, but I do know that stillness was more his enemy than a welcomed friend.

A LOYAL COMPANION

As a child, I anticipated the thrill of scaling up the T-formation that provided shape and form to our clothesline pole. I was familiar with its rough, porous texture. Its color was a part of my personality—green. I spent my summer with this friend as I hung upside down on its extended arm of support. This became my first love, as I frequently dated this place. While I freely hung upside down from its comfort, I didn't always know where it began and I ended. It's like a marriage for me; the two have become one.

When I was there, nothing clouded my understanding. I forgot the life that existed within the four walls of the home that sat within the same boundaries of my parents' city lot. I breathed, I thought, I rested—and peace washed over my young soul, which raced to understand the ups and downs of living with imperfect people, myself included.

My time hanging on that pole was where I learned about the gift of lingering. It's where new life emerged. I felt restored like the earth does when rain has been gifted from the skies. Yes, my soul was colored green like the spring grasses.

I knew when my date with this loyal companion was over and my time to hang had expired. Not because I looked at a watch or followed some ritual created, but because my mental clarity and perspective burst forth. I lingered in silence. I waited for the waltz of my soul to indicate the end of my heart's dance with solitude. It's time. With the skill of an acrobat, I flipped off and scored a perfect landing on the ground beneath. Life awaited my return, and I was now ready to reenter.

TWO FACES OF LINGERING

Lingering, and its many synonyms—remaining, surviving, persisting, and abiding—have two very different faces.

One face smiles when the circumstance of our life brings pleasure. We grasp to hold onto the joy and delight that a quiet summer's evening can bring. We inhale the smell of a newborn baby and impress our face into their soft and supple skin. The kind embrace of one who loves us when we are most unlovable and reminds us that "till death do we part" really matters. The smell of bread baking in the oven, wafting up the aroma of yeast chemically interacting with the simple elements mixed in. We want to stand in those moments and drink in the life-giving force they grant. These moments of delight resonate with our innate desire to live simple and pure. They give shape to our lives and remind us that life has a tender side.

The other face of lingering grimaces. Pain has arrived

and doesn't indicate its departure date. We scratch and claw at its presence as we try to avoid the time pain requires of us. We demand its removal. Pain has its own agenda, and with a staunch determination it refuses to take one step in an opposing direction. Instead, pain defiantly moves toward us. The more we run from its advancing agenda, the more life territory it invades.

This is when lingering converts to surviving. Survival demands immediate use of all our acquired life skills and the creation of skills not yet available or developed. It's in these moments we will either languish or develop. The difference is in the choosing. The choosing is ours and not some cosmic, random selection.

No one taught us how to experience pain. It's like the dance I cannot do. I don't know how, so it's better to exit the dance floor and away from pain's emo sounds. But my exit from learning the dance of pain only incapacitates me the next time pain requires my hand.

What is required is that I take the hand offered and learn the steps. When I no longer feel the awkwardness of dancing with an unfamiliar partner and I've lingered long enough to understand the moves pain requires, I'll know I've arrived. Only when I've completed pain's dance card will it excuse itself and exit the dance floor of my life.

Lingering is a gift many people pass off as an

imposition that impedes their final life destination. However, to linger is not an impediment to our life's final port but rather a necessary harbor to anchor into and learn the finer points of dancing with pain.

Living balanced through pain requires us to make the difficult decision to abide in its presence. Pain teaches us how to live our lives more fully, because it teaches us the steps we must take to be poised, kind, and compassionate human beings.

A TABLET ISN'T GOOD ENOUGH

When I served as a school nurse, I encountered many eager children who sought me out with the complaint of a headache, in anticipation of a quick fix to their pain. I thwarted many students by requiring them to answer a few simple questions. "Have you eaten this morning? Have you had any water today? How long have you had your headache? Do you wear glasses? What time did you go to bed last night?" On and on my questions would go. I knew something they didn't understand. Relieving the pain with a tablet wouldn't solve the problem. Yes, it would perhaps alleviate their subjective report of pain, but it wouldn't pinpoint the cause of the pain and teach them how to avoid or deal with the pain should it return. They were asking me to make the pain go away. I was asking them to linger and answer my questions. The answer to these questions would be the foundation for me to teach them and their learning what brought the pain and, perhaps, how to thwart its return.

Lingering in our pain develops us as human beings as we become fully aware of the life God has gifted us with, and we begin to develop the attributes of a God who is both holy and righteous. Lingering provides life lessons that no other emotion or experience can provide. It paints our life with color and enriches our capacity to love, feel, and pose ourselves to fulfill our life purpose and arrive at our final destination.

Lingering frees us from distraction and captures our full attention. It allows us to narrow our focus and extend care to our own souls. We waste so much time flailing around in our busyness, hoping pain won't find an entrance. What we deny is that it already has entered into the threshold of our lives and won't go unnoticed or go away until we give it the time it bids. We will either learn from pain or relinquish our rights to its gifts and walk blindly in our ignorance.

TOUCHED BY LIFE

I was also a nursing instructor for several years. This job afforded me the pleasure of teaching my craft to eager students and to enjoy the company of people seeking comfort and solace. On one particular day, I assigned a man with terminal cancer to my student. Knowing this would give her an opportunity to learn from the dying, I entered his room to make introductions.

His distraught wife and daughter were off to the side, engaged in a discussion of options to keep their loved one anchored to this vanishing existence we call life. I introduced myself to these women and then went straight to my target, the patient. I was my usual polite self as I introduced both myself and his student nurse.

After our introduction, I asked the patient's permission to have a student oversee his care. In his weakened state he politely complied with my request. His eyes were tender. He exuded a characteristic about him that implied he had lived and understood life in a way that most people don't, and I was unknowingly going to be part of his sharing of the knowledge he was ready to bequeath anyone willing. I was willing.

With a weak voice, this kind man asked if I had a few minutes to talk. Sensing urgency in his request, I asked if I could sit with him on his bed. My request was granted. My student sat in a chair to his side, and for the next thirty minutes—the room filled with people and activity—I listened as he gave me the gift of his life. Eyes focused and hearts connected, I heard about a man who loved his childhood. He'd served as a cook in the military; he'd loved cooking. I said nothing but allowed the pain of his impending death to shower me with blessings from a life well-lived through both pain and pleasure. For those moments I'd mentally emptied the room and refused to allow the fullness to distract.

I wasn't touching death—I was being touched by life. That is the gift of pain. Pain has a life-giving quality that we miss when we seek to eliminate its presence prematurely. Pain allows us to pare down if we are willing to say yes and sit with it.

In the weeks and months that followed my dad's suicide, I simply had nothing left to offer friends, colleagues, or extended family. I chose to withdraw from unnecessary commitments and simply perform the tasks of mothering and marriage. I changed my status to part-time at work and made no room for the myriad of people who had relied upon me to provide counsel and assistance. I had a choice. I was either going to sit with pain and listen or run while it chased me endlessly. I chose to sit and linger.

When we linger in the pain produced by life tilts, it blesses us and others.

At the conclusion of our time together, with death

waiting its turn, this dying man looked at me with a smile of completion and stated, "Thanks, I needed that. I couldn't get them to listen." He gestured toward his wife and daughter. I often think about this man's family. I wonder how different their final moments would have been if they would have made the choice to surrender and linger in the presence of his dying.

He died that day. Later, his wife brought in a plastic grocery bag filled with some of his favorite cooking magazines. She explained to me that he wanted me to have them.

When I look at these magazines, I am reminded what his family lost and what I gleaned from the field of his life in review. I was willing to linger with death knocking, but death did not have the final word. This man's life keeps reproducing fruit in my life, as his pain of departing taught me how to be still and listen. In listening, I learned how to live with people as my priority. Pain teaches us how to live with compassion toward those who are hurting as we understand the sting of being hurt. We judge less because pain reminds us that all of humanity is frail and seeking solace in the company of frailty. We are not weak in our frailty. We're weak in our refusal to accept or acknowledge our fragile state. Running from pain is where our brittle souls begin to crack and will often break. Pain is our tensile strength, because it reinforces us with reminders of what is important and lasting and presents questions that, when thoughtfully answered, propel us forward.

LEARNING FROM SUFFERING

The more we linger in the pain of our life tilts, the more we loosen our grip on unnecessary and unfruitful activities that were never intended to define our identity or direct us toward our life design and how we were created to serve in this world.

Befriending pain illuminates our weaknesses and our strengths. It challenges our belief systems and drains the uninvited and useless distractions. Once these distractions are removed, we can more clearly see the foundation we've built our life upon.

Pain is God's way of testing this foundation we've blindly accepted as unfailing. We'll only begin to loosen our grip on these fruitless beliefs, activities, and pursuits once we see the reality of how debilitated our foundation is.

I often wonder what pain my dad was running from. Whatever it was, it caught up with him on that fateful day. I think about how different his life may have ended if he would have taken the hand of pain and learned how to dance the dance of sorrow and loss. What life lessons did he miss? Was his inability to stay and visit friends and family his life metaphor for not wanting to relate to pain? Pain is a relationship, and like all relationships, we accept the benefits and challenges.

It's where we choose to linger, either in the challenges or in the benefits, which determines the outcome of any relationship. When we linger with pain, we must choose to linger in its benefits or we will never see it as the friend we need.

Every decision leads to a destination. When we choose to circumvent pain's presence, we forfeit the fullness of a meaningful life. We become so busy running that we land in a desolate place that we get duped into believing is our real destination. When we can no longer endure the parched soul that running from pain creates, we'll be faced with a decision that will determine what we will serve.

September 10, 2007, six-and-a-half weeks after my dad's suicide, I wrote in my journal:

I want to scream! What is it others don't know—can't know? What is it I am to know? To what exclusive club do I belong—for members only—where the members are living in isolation like me? I did not ask to join–member by association. Will I serve my suffering with meaning, or will the meaning suffer? Father, teach me to suffer with meaning. Help me to serve this teacher responsibly.

In other words, help me to live responsibly with the lesson that suffering has to teach. Let the purpose be the language I learn from this uninvited guest.

We have a responsibility to pain, as with any guest, invited or not. We surrender. Surrender illuminates our path to God's greater purpose. It accepts pain as the pen that God uses to complete our life stories. When we refuse to sit with pain, we forget how to be a student, and the lesson of pain will be wasted. Perhaps a part of our soul will also emaciate.

I am reminded of Job, a man who God allowed to walk in an amount of grief and loss that perhaps no modern-day person has ever had to experience. Job, a devout man who lived thousands of years ago, lost everything: children, property, wealth, and his health. For reasons unknown to Job, he had to choose how he would manage his pain, anxiety, and great despair that these losses created. Why would God allow a man who was so committed to living righteously to suffer?

Job strips and prostrates himself upon an ash heap to express his grief and to make sense of the senseless. With incomplete and distorted knowledge, Job's friends join him to question the why of pain. Question after question is asked, but the silence of God continues. Job's friends want to make a quick assessment for the reason of his pain, so they conclude that Job must be guilty of some grievous sin that brought down God's cosmic wrath. Who doesn't want to rush pain away with an answer, even if the answer leads to the wrong conclusion? Wrong conclusions, however, lead to wrong decisions. And wrong decisions lead to more pain, because we tend to build our lives around what we conclude to be truth "evidenced" by default. But Job, as he pleaded his innocence before his accusers, didn't appear to want to rush and make the wrong conclusion. So he sat and lingered in the presence of God's silence. His lingering did not imply his resignation to forfeit an answer or to seek understanding of the reasons behind the losses. He was willing to wait for them, despite his pain.

Job became weaker and weaker as he wrestled in the presence of a silent God. He submitted question after question to God, his anguish made evident when he said things like, "I cry out to You for help, but You don't answer me. I stand up, and You turn Your attention against me" (Job 30:20). What Job didn't yet know or understand, was that God was working in the silence that pain created. The silence of pain always birth life if we are willing to linger in its presence. Job is about to experience the freshness of life that lingering brings.

As the story of Job comes to a climax, we get a ringside seat as we hear how God breaks through the silence and rewards Job for his willingness to wait in the tomb of pain. Perhaps it's not the answer we expect, but it is the answer that Job requires in order to see the fullness of God. Instead of answering Job's questions, God required Job to answer *His* questions. Is this not what pain purposes, for us to be accountable to the questions?

Job is forced to hear questions about God's perfect, sovereign design. Can Job withstand the questions of a holy God demanding he answer? Is Job able to answer the questions about how God created everything and the reason and purpose behind His creation? Can any of us?

But God is gracious and uses his questions only as a way to reveal the truth behind Job 42:2. "I know that You can do all things, and that no purpose of Yours can be thwarted." Furthermore, Job reveals an important lesson that lingering provides. "I have heard of You by the hearing of the ear; but now my eye sees You" (verse 5).

God does not condemn Job for asking questions about things he knows little to nothing about. Rather, He simply corrects Job's misconceptions about who controls the universe and how God can choose to use, at His disposal, any tool He desires to inscribe meaning and purpose into our lives. Job now had an understanding of life that lingering in pain provided. He now sees God, not in the literal sense of seeing with the eyes but figuratively seeing God with the heart.

When we can begin to understand God within our heart, we can understand that there is no pain that can enter our life that God is not able to use. He's able to remove the false premises and beliefs about life that we've built our careers, families, friendships, and lives upon. God desires for us to walk sure-footed and steady, and we can only live the balanced life once our faulty foundations have been toppled.

The reward of lingering with pain as our gifted teacher is a life renewed with abundance. God restored to Job twofold of what he'd lost. Job 42:17 tells us that "Job died, an old man and full of days." Perhaps God will not restore what has been lost through our life tilts, but our joy can return—the joy of knowing God's intentions toward us are good and that the lesson behind pain is one of a life lived with meaning. The fullness of His presence will erase the doubt of our existence that life tilts call to question. Lingering has a destination, and we must be willing to wait in expectation.

FAMILIAR MUSIC

Although my dad never mastered the art of lingering, his life and his death taught me about how to linger in the dance we call life. Without knowing, he participated in teaching me how to live. He took my hand and we danced together. It was awkward at first, even painful.

Eventually, I began to understand where his life was taking me. Instead of fighting with his steps and direction, I decided to surrender and learn. My dad didn't finish our dance or our time together as father and daughter, but I will finish it for us both. I will remember our time together and continue to learn how to dance to life's rhythm. At times I will dance alone, but the presence of God will be my instructor and perhaps even my partner. I will linger and then live.

The next time you are on the dance floor of life, linger. Watch in silence, if you must, as those who've learned to dance—by the art of lingering—step in rhythm to the music.

You, too, will one day learn what your next step is when your hand is requested by life's tilts. The music will become familiar, and you'll understand its purpose. Hold close any relationships and tilts God desires to use to point your gaze toward His sovereign will and the completion of your life.

Trust in the life that lingering produces. Like any dance, the music ends and we leave the floor refreshed and filled with joy. When it's time, you'll know to leave its presence and journey forward.

Linger, dance, and live, for this is the gift of life tilts.

Living balanced means choosing to linger in the gifts pain leaves and not in the loss pain creates.

Chapter 7

Release

Grace is the beauty of form under the influence of freedom.
Friedrich Schiller

THE FALL

Young hearts don't believe old bodies can keep up with the physical agility and zest of the adolescent. This went through my mind when my dad insisted on going roller skating with me one Friday night when I was in high school. The skating rink was my place of solace. I spent four nights a week there skating—really, escaping. I honed the skills of spinning, jumping, and learning how to skate backward in a circle. My confidence grew as my skills increased. Now my intoxicated dad wanted to invade my space and demonstrate his skills.

Hesitantly, I agreed to take him. My dad was unusually conversational on the ride to the rink. He recalled his glory days as a speed demon on quads and his ability to dance and "jig" on four wheels. By the time we arrived at the rink, I was convinced that this man, who I was faintly acquainted with, could teach me more about the craft of roller skating than hours of practice had provided.

My motivation was kindled as I selfishly determined the goal and outcome of our impending time together in my mind—I could become an all-star skater.

We donned our skates. By the time we emerged onto the wooden floor, it was obvious that I and others had their doubts as to my dad's ability to stay in an upright position. Torn between wanting to skate ahead and practice my usual skating calisthenics or dutifully stay with my dad, I decided it would be better for both me and him to forfeit my desire for a future in the Olympics and serve his benefit as a roller-skating aide.

Slowly and cautiously, we began our first lap around the rink. The young skate guard made his way through the youthful crowd and politely offered his assistance. Because my dad's unsteadiness was obvious, he wanted to ensure both his safety and the safety of the other skaters.

I sheepishly shook my head "no thank you," but my heart was pleading for him to stay close by. He recognized my desire for his presence and lingered for a few seconds. With a questioning nod for his permission to leave, I once again released him from any paid obligation. My selfish desire to lose myself in my weekly oasis gave way to my dad's safety. Back and forth my mind and body went, trying to decide if I should reach out and take his arm or allow him the dignity of the man he was so proud to be. I decided to guard his manliness and gently submit to his presence on the floor.

Within minutes, all my hesitation and concern for my father's safety was validated. My first bolt of adrenaline rushed in as he began to reach his arms forward to steady his wobbly legs. His feet began to falter on the wooden floor like staccato notes played on the piano, and before I could reach out and grab him, he lay sprawled on the rink's floor like a newborn foal birthed onto the earth's surface.

I waved oncoming skaters away as I reached to assist my dad back into an upright position. The friendly guard dashed to my side and provided assistance. Between the two of us, we successfully hoisted my dad off the floor. My dad guarded his elbow while insisting he was okay, so we began skating again—with greater caution. Soon he mentioned our short stay on the floor was enough, relinquished his right as the decision maker, and followed me off the floor.

Helpless, my dad allowed me to assist him with removing his skates and donning his shoes. The employees at the rink allowed us to leave with our dignity intact and bid us farewell.

We engaged in small talk on our drive home. My father was embarrassed and defeated in his attempt to spend quality time with me, so I assured him that our time spent had been meaningful. My foremost concern was his elbow, so I switched the conversation and encouraged him to consider seeing a physician. Later that evening my mother took him to the emergency room and had his arm X-rayed. He had fractured his elbow.

"I LOVE YOU TOO"

Since my dad had retired, he called often. Some days my heart grinned, even though my eyes may have rolled, at the many calls. I gladly answered and took delight in our verbal exchange. Today, his voice sounded surprisingly euphoric.

It was early evening, so I was under pressure to get dinner on the table and tend to the multitude of tasks of a working mother and wife. As I listened, his words and tone came across as a man who may have recently been freed from a lifelong prison term. His spirit bounced at me like a fully inflated ball. He seemed childlike as he joyfully shared about something he'd recently done. There was a confessional theme behind his many words as he filled in the details.

My father entertained me with his anecdotal narratives for about twenty minutes. With carefully chosen words, I assured my dad I would call him the next day to talk more about his recent exploits. In typical form, I expressed my love to my father. What was atypical was the sense of urgency to make sure he heard me with his heart and not just his ears. Again, with greater emphasis and passion, I punctuated the words. "Dad, I love you. You know that, don't you?"

His response was light. "Yes, I know. I love you too."

I smiled, believing he did comprehend the depth of my love for him. I wanted him to sense the forgiveness I was extending to him for being a distant father while I was growing up. His alcohol addiction had rendered him incapable of forming a bond with me, and I needed him to know we were now united as father and daughter regardless of our past together.

Although these wouldn't be the last words I'd hear from him, they would be the last words he heard from me.

The next day, my dad spoke his final words—the ones that have been permanently etched in my heart and mind.

With my dad forever gone, I spent months and years replaying that final phone conversation between father and daughter. I rehearsed each word, analyzed them for clues that could provide answers to my continual onslaught of questions.

Under the scrutiny of my interrogator-accuser-self, I convinced myself I had missed the evidence of a man ready to pull the trigger and end his life. Clearly, he'd called me to reach out, to stop him, and I, unknowingly, denied his need during the last hours of his life. He was asking me to serve him his final meal of relational food, and I had returned his plate empty.

Tormented by his death, I rewrote my dad's final chapter. Convinced I possessed some magical powers to rewrite history, I rehearsed my new scripts for sustaining his life on a daily basis.

If I'd visited more often, he would have felt supported. I shouldn't have rolled my eyes at his endless emails that validated the sleepless nights that he spent pursuing the Internet for silly jokes to alleviate the mental and emotional despair he hid so well. Why didn't I purchase the neighbor's house with the mother-in-law addition for him and my mom to live in? Why did I attribute his ongoing comments of, "I don't know how much more of this I can take," to a predictable statement people growing older make when faced with failing health and declining youth. Had I failed to effectively convey my love and forgiveness?

My mind crafted more accusations while my heart and

soul absorbed them as infallible truths. Endlessly, my mind played out all the new additions to his life script as I had rewritten it, and in the end I convinced myself that my dad had lived.

I needed him to live, as I needed absolution of what I believed to be my relational omissions and neglect of duties and responsibilities as his daughter.

Without realizing what my newly concocted accusations and rewritten narrative had achieved, I had taken ownership of his choice and subsequent outcome.

I believed that my lack of ability to control the situation was my fault. I imagined my poor choices to be the finger that pulled the trigger and delivered the fatal bullet. Forensics would not find my fingerprints on his gun, but I believed the heavens would shout, "Guilty! Guilty!" Yes, I had concluded that my dad was dead due to some failure on my part to act on his behalf.

THE MYTH OF CONTROL

Life tilts have a way of leading to faulty thinking. They take us down mental paths that create a belief system. This system empowers us to believe that we possess the ability to change life outcomes for the people we love and care for. We grip onto their life choices like a punctured jugular vein. We believe saving people from the consequences of their choices is our responsibility.

So we plan, attempt to predict the outcomes of our plans, and convince ourselves we are God. We believe our loved one's agreement and allegiance to our plan is what will save them from their emotional, spiritual, and mental separation from peace and joy. What we fail to understand, though, is we drown out our own peace and joy. Now, two people are down, not one.

My belief in the power to save lives comes from being trained as a registered nurse. I am confronted with choices that bear outcomes for those who entrust their lives to the medical profession every day. Hence, I saw saving my father as my responsibility—at least that's what I unrealistically came to believe. Slowly, I came to understand that I had built the idea that I could save my dad on quicksand and accepted that my dad's outcome belonged solely to him and not me. Accepting this became my gift.

The gift of a life tilt is the ability to peel back our false belief about what we have the ability to control within our lives. Tilts reconfigure our thinking and remove the false confidence in ourselves that leads to incompetent and irresponsible living. We have no control over circumstances and events or over another human being, regardless of age, gender, demographics, or socioeconomic status.

Babies cry in their time frame. Boys and girls

inherently display temperaments that either play into or against our pleasure or displeasure. Poverty exists whether or not we give generously to relief organizations. Abuse occurs in spite of laws protecting the abused and our efforts to protect. Tornadoes, snowstorms, lightning strikes, and all other ordered and ordained phenomenon happen in spite of any preplanning and prepping I do.

I never have had, don't today, and never will possess or exert control external to my being. Neither do you. This is the lesson of a life tilt.

What we all do possess and have control over is the power to influence our world and those living within our reach. We can all reach out to extend positive encouragement and discourse, and sometime we may even touch a life directly with our words and actions.

However, there will be times when in our reaching, we don't touch the seat of humanity and impact change, but we must continue to reach. Influencing is more about our willingness to reach even if our touch is not received or effective. There's a vast difference between control and influence, as you will come to understand.

Control demands change to occur after we've spent time and energy reaching out to assist people. We insist our efforts and good intentions be met without resistance and that people should be compelled to joyfully extend gratitude based on the outcomes we've manipulated and stamped as well-fit for the person and his or her circumstance.

But, demanding conformity is destructive to relationships, because it chokes out the life force that giving-and-taking in a relationship fosters. Each person in a relationship is both a teacher and a learner. There is beauty in this exchange, because dependence is fostered.

The times we are the teacher, purpose and meaning is birthed. As a learner, we have the support and security of someone coming alongside of us and offering guidance.

But prideful control rejects the notion that learning is equal, or perhaps superior, to teaching. This rejection to become the learner and need to control through our teaching is based on fear.

Fear compels the controller to believe that personal needs can be met, failure can be avoided, criticism can be thwarted, disappointment can be abandoned, and rejection is capable of being disabled from our psyche.

Control equates to happiness and serenity, or so we naively think. But when we come to the end of our days, beaten and bruised, we realize we were scourged by the whip of control and we were the ones handling the whip.

At its inception, control is lack of trust. A trust that believes pain, hardships, disorder, tears, emptiness, and dark moments within our soul are designed for our good. That God has ordered our days and inscribed our experiences as part of His sovereign plan. Absent from one who desires to control is a trust in God's mercy and grace as sufficient for the darkest experience, regardless the length of that darkness.

The moment we fail to trust God for deliverance when we're in our painful life tilts is when we anchor ourselves to control and maneuver ourselves to avoid the pain of living in a fallen world. We categorize and compartmentalize life into "things that cause pain" and "ways to control or avoid things that cause pain."

We believe our system works and that controlling outcomes is more efficient than trusting God in the wait through pain. We distrust the metamorphosis of painful confinement, disbelieving that beauty exists at the end of the trail pain paved.

Control doesn't trust God for our identity and fears what can happen when identity is relinquished to God's sovereignty. As a parent, I often attempted to control the actions and decisions of my daughters. Falsely I believed that my control was for their good and safety, and in some respects my intentions were pure.

But, when my anger flared over the choices my daughters made that I did not approve of, I realized I had tethered my identity to both their choices and their outcomes.

Control believes we can design our identity by manipulating outcomes. Good parenting equals well-behaved children and, therefore, will reflect my flawless character.

We desire to personify perfection in a fallen world that points fingers of criticism in order to deflect lives of imperfection. Imperfection has become a disease, and control is the cure. The lie behind this is that we retain the power to create and protect our self-imposed identity by manipulating outcomes. The truth is, we relinquish our power to the opinions of people when we find our identity in the choices others make. The decisions another person makes don't define us; they define them.

INFLUENCE GIVES LIFE

On December 15, 2007 at 7:24 p.m., I wrote in my journal:

I am not to tie my destiny into another's choice. I must quit compromising my God-ordained call to alleviate _____'s chosen outcomes. I am not responsible for _____'s choices. Father, release me. Teach me to sing the song of the called and not the dirge of one shackled. Freedom is my lyric.

Control also doesn't wait. It doesn't believe that change is possible if we surrender people and circumstances to God and wait for Him to decide when to deliver the outcomes that are best suited to propel us and others forward in life.

We're seduced to believe that God's perfect plan has an expiration date. Because we hate expiration dates, we become the author of our life outcomes and secure God a backseat to our lives. After all, we believe that if God's plans have expired, then they were second best to our conviction that our plan has no expiration date and is foolproof.

What we fail to understand is that God is infinite in His existence and power, while we are finite. In essence, we're the ones with an expiration date. When we die, our plans die with us. God's plans live forever, even when death requires our presence.

In the end, control is ultimately life's greatest thief. It steals our time, energy, and ability to live as influencers. Wayne Muller, in his book *A Life of Being, Having, and Doing Enough*, writes:

> *How much of our time is driven by our conviction that we somehow have the authority, the power, the audacity to believe that if we anticipate, plan, work hard and long enough, and take care of everything and everyone, then*

we can actually control the outcome or guarantee the success of what we have decided we want.[1]

The time we so willingly spend to control outcomes outside of our reach is time we foolishly exchange for other life choices, ones we actually control and that impact real outcomes.

We use time irresponsibly when we attempt to control the choices others make. We cannot. We also can't control the state of our country or believe that our anxiety over the evil acts of kings and rulers changes their decisions. We demand comfort, conformity, and predictability, so we demand control. But instead of control, we have expended precious, limited time given by God.

Wisdom is remembering that any time spent trying to alter choices imposed upon us by others is simply time wasted; it will be locked six feet under when the earth clothes us in a final salute.

It's to our advantage to review our lives and remember the events and relationships that once parched our soul while we clawed for control. Are these people and events as influential as we once believed? Will they be ten years from this moment? Is this investment of our time and personal reserves worth the withdrawal upon our life's finite time and energy?

As we grab and claw for control over the

uncontrollable, the less quality of life and freedom we experience and the more out of control our inner world becomes.

Our time is much better spent living authentically and fully aware of our power to influence today. Influence is based on a foundation of trust and respect. Trust is believing that the decision acted upon by another doesn't limit your ability to act and respond with wisdom and prudence in any given circumstance or situation.

Respect is granted to the decision maker, regardless of mutual agreement or belief, and acts as a preserver of the relationship because it accepts and rests in the unknown.

The power of influence rests in its many positive, life-giving characteristics.

Influence is present-oriented. It understands the need to make choices that need to be made given the circumstances. It doesn't predict the outcome of those choices but rather trusts that the decision is made with integrity, honesty, and purity of heart. When decisions are made based on the power of influence, relationships are nurtured because influence is others-oriented.

Value and kindness are part of the character of influence and enable the influencer to cast a vision, instill purpose, and ignite passion upon those who abide in the sphere of the influencer.

Influence is grace in action. How we perceive people and events is the difference between control and influence. Control demands strict obedience to standards, predetermined by both man and society. Influence grants grace to the standards that Christ hung on a cross to redeem. Influence recognizes the fallibility of mankind and grants freedom and margin for failure to do its work.

The strength of influence lies in our ability to respond with forgiveness and understanding. Influencers accept their flawed nature and extend grace and mercy toward events and people that demonstrate the same flawed qualities inherent in all of creation. Influence leads by compassion because it looks in the mirror and sees brokenness in need of healing.

MEANINGFUL, PURPOSEFUL

History is abundant with stories about influencers who freely led with elements of grace, kindness, forgiveness, and compassion. One such story is found in Viktor Frankl's vivid recount of living through the dysfunction of World War II, found in his book *Man's Search for Meaning.* He conveys how influence has the ability to overcome evil.

His book concentrates on mankind's responses to circumstances and portrays the power of influence in the midst of horrific events both witnessed and endured.

Frankl conveys that he stood stripped of all he once held close, including body hair. In one moment of clarity, he decided that nothing outside of him could dictate his internal locus of control—man's power to influence his circumstances by his ability to choose his response to evil. He conveys this clearly when he writes:

> *The experiences of camp life show that man does have a choice of action. Man can preserve a vestige of spiritual freedom, of independence of mind, even in such terrible conditions of psychic and physical stress. They [examples] may have been few in number, but they offer sufficient proof that everything can be taken from a man but one thing: the last of human freedoms—to choose one's attitude in any given set of circumstances.*[2]

Frankl demonstrates that the power of influence lies in the ability to choose one's attitude regardless of a situation or its outcome. He recounts the daily choices that each inmate had to make in the midst of such cruel deprivation. He was witness to men who, in the midst of their own personal suffering, "walked through the huts comforting others, giving away their last piece of bread." Frankl supports his observations further as he writes:

> *And there were always choices to make. Every day, every*

hour, offered the opportunity to make a decision, a decision which determined whether you would or would not submit to those powers which threatened to rob you of your very self, your inner freedom; which determined whether or not you would become the plaything of circumstance, renouncing freedom and dignity to become molded into the form of the typical inmate . . . in the final analysis it becomes clear that the sort of person the prisoner became was the result of an inner decision, and not the result of camp influence alone. Fundamentally, therefore, any man can, even under such circumstances, decide what shall become of him—mentally and spiritually. It's this spiritual freedom—which cannot be taken away—that makes life meaningful and purposeful.

As demonstrated through this historical account, we see that the power of influence rests in its purpose. Influence purposes to grant freedom, under the influence of both granting and receiving grace.

Influence is freedom. Freedom to trust, to believe, to hope that in the end all things bring glory to God, regardless of any decision I do or don't make. It's seeing with new eyes. It's growth found in rest. When we rest in the unfinished work of life, we gain insight and understanding. The gain of influence surpasses the confining space of control.

YOUR OWN LIFE STORY

I think back to my dad's broken elbow. To the time on that wooden floor in the skate rink when a young girl and skate guard doubted the wisdom of a middle-aged, drunken man's presence. Years later, I realize had I attempted to force a different decision on my father and rewrite history, my personal pain would have increased, not decreased.

My dad's decision to skate meant he was present with me instead of absent. What I experienced was relationship, and it would cost a broken bone to pave this path of father and daughter, parent and child. In that moment, my dad and I were right where we were supposed to be. Together, we made a memory that would last the length of both our lives.

Often, with great pleasure, I've been able to recount that night and smile, because my dad and I took a step forward in our relationship. His elbow healed, and my heart took one step forward toward healing.

On Friday, July 27, 2007 at 1:15 p.m., I was right where I was supposed to be—on the phone with my parents as my dad spoke his last words. What I once believed to be barren sand became fertile ground for God to expand my understanding of Him. Brokenness precedes healing, and it's only when healing is necessary that the glory of God is magnified and relationship is entered. What looked like unfinished work on the day my dad died became the pen through which purpose was written and birthed.

My dad's death opened up paths to relating with people in pain across this country. Like Job, my life tilt became the moment I could say, "I have heard of You, God, but now the eyes of my heart and soul really do see You" (Job 42:5).

What I came to see is that life tilts pave the way for personal growth and understanding if we are willing to relinquish the need to control, rewrite, rehearse, and script another's life story. I could not have seen that before my dad's untimely death.

People need the freedom to write their own life story, even to their detriment. It doesn't mean I can't utilize the power of influence. Rather, I must love them as is and allow influence to seep deeply into their hearts and souls. Whatever a person chooses reflects the core of who they are, not who you or I am. We must remember that allowing people to make their own choices is the moment compassion and kindness is ushered in and influence can do its work.

Jesus is a good example of offering life principles to live by and allowing people to either step toward Him or away from Him. Jesus neither controlled nor owned the choices of those He loved. He simply made Himself available to hurting, marginalized, broken, and sinful people. The gift He gave to each person was the power to choose whether or not he or she would step toward the gifts of healing and salvation. Never did Jesus walk away offended or wounded at the choice each person made. He was never defined by the outcomes or choices made by others. And because He detached Himself from others' outcomes, it allowed Him to move forward and complete the work of His assigned ministry. I wonder how often the lifework we have been given is halted because we take on the ownership of decisions and the subsequent outcomes that don't belong to us?

Our life's mission cannot be reduced by someone else's decision that bleeds over into our lives. Jesus' life mission was completed the moment His death sentence was handed down and nails were pounded into His innocent hands. Like Jesus, our life mission will also move toward completion when we choose to detach from decisions and outcomes that don't belong to us and we offer others the freedom to our influence and not the choking death grip our control creates.

FREEDOM TO GIVE HEALING

After my dad's suicide, I, like Viktor Frankl, would have to choose where my power belonged—in my father's tragic death, or in my ability to step back and decide my response? Life tilts don't take away our purpose; they lead to purpose. They don't take away the meaning of our existence but rather enrich the meaning behind our lives. When we lose the chains of control, we realize that nothing happens to us. Rather, it happens for us.

God purposes our life with meaning, and life tilts are often the road He uses to create that meaning. Our part is to accept His creative plan as He weaves hope into each day. God assures us in Isaiah 14:24, 27 that "as I have planned, so it will it be, and as I have purposed, so it will happen . . . For the Lord Almighty has purposed, and who can thwart Him? His hand is stretched out, and who can turn it back?"

There is nothing and no one, no decision, no misstep, no choice that enters our life that God has not purposed in advance, so our life tilts come at the moment God intends. We won't enjoy the moments these tilts enter into our lives—I didn't—but we must embrace them as a gift if we're going to live full lives filled with hope and expectation.

Expectation opens our hearts to look for opportunities to grow and develop fully into the person God has designed. His holy intention is good. When we embrace the goodness of this intention is when we can rise above the pain and be defined by Him and not by our tilted world. God's use of life tilts illuminates our soul and awakens our spirit to become the person God intends for us to be today and the one we are capable of becoming tomorrow.

We are responsible for the moments life tilts create. We must realize that every step in our tilts is necessary, and we can choose to learn from them. We'll walk with wobbly legs and hesitant steps. We'll cry, grimace, our hearts will grow faint, and our spirit will dry up. But we can choose to take the next step in the presence of these life-giving and teachable moments.

What each person does with their life tilts determines this moment, and this moment designs the next. Moments turn into days and days into a life. Each decision you make while you're in a life tilt will either thrust you into a gorge where personal injury is imminent and walking death is possible, or the decision will open up opportunities for life to be birthed and tears turned into triumph. Life tilts summon forth decisions, and as the writer of Deuteronomy challenges, we should make decisions that will give life for both us and those under our care (Deuteronomy 30:15, 19).

Our freedom to influence and not to control is the difference between spiritual and relational life and death.

Now, I'm living freely and enjoying the freedom of

being detached from my father's personal choice and the story he decided to write for himself. This decision to detach from the outcomes of his decision has propelled me forward in life and allowed me the freedom to take control over the areas of my life that belong to me.

As I trust God to sovereignly control whatever outcomes are attached to the decisions others make, I'm available to exert more influence into their lives and various circumstances. And although my dad's choice follows me each day, I have chosen to live in the gifts his final life decision gave to me. Though my tears continue, they are rivers of life and no longer the sorrow of false guilt. Because I chose to live.

Today, give yourself the same gift and detach from decisions other people make. When you do, you will foster a life-giving force that will propel you forward in life and allow you the freedom to exert influence.

Living balanced means being willing to relinquish the need to control, rewrite, and rehearse a different life story.

Chapter 8

The Gravity of Gratitude

I saw grief drinking a cup of sorrow and called out,
"It tastes sweet, does it not?"
"You've caught me," grief answered, "and you've
ruined my business, how can I sell sorrow when you
know it's a blessing?"
Jalaluddin Rumi

OUR MOMENT

My dad's presence is calm, relaxed, unusually inviting, unlike the celebration of this Independence Day I am surrounded by. I sit next to a man who seems like he has answered life's demanding questions. He's become a sage in his own manner. I don't want to leave his side, fearing I'll miss some wisdom he seems so desirous to impart. There is much I can learn from him, so I linger.

Family and friends are gathered on the back porch of my brother's home. I feel obliged to offer small visits with each person who has come to partake in this night of celebration on my behalf. I go between small talk with family and acquaintances and looking back to make sure he hasn't left. He remains seated, willing to sit patiently and await my return. He exudes a confidence that I will indeed return. His confidence is not misplaced.

Years have lapsed since the celebration of my parents' twenty-fifth wedding anniversary. This time my family is gathered to celebrate my twenty-fifth wedding anniversary.

I draw my chair closer to him. I smell the sweetness of his skin and see that his advancing years haven't stripped it of its soft and supple characteristic. It's the softness I will always remember.

On this summer evening, I feel an attraction toward a man I have grown to understand better. I've watched him morph and become someone who shelters people rather than scorches them out of his personal pain and torment. Today I'm not worried about this man lashing out at me or making me the object of his judgment. He now shelters me, his gestures kind as he wears a tender smile. The years between my childhood and my adulthood have erased my fear of this man.

As the night progresses, I sense he, too, is drawn toward me. I am restless, but he assures me the evening will work out and winks. The crowd is calling me to come away from my father, forcing me to give up this remarkable moment to praise the silver wedding cake that's been purchased for this day.

I surrender to the safety of his presence. I begin to understand this is his gift.

I'm grateful for this moment, as it erases the years he spent emotionally and mentally avoiding me.

The crowd calls me to partake of the cake and listen to the cacophony of singing "Happy Anniversary." Reluctantly, I get up and pretend I'm enraptured by this marital celebration. I am not. I'm only captured by the audience of one—my dad. I look at him with assurance and say I'll come back to stay by his side until night or sleep pulls us apart.

He smiles and nods. I have never experienced this peace he now radiates. I want to know his secret—the transformative power. He will disclose this to me in twenty-three summer days.

He is gone. His peace is now my pain.

RECITING WHAT REMAINS

Quietly I look over the calm water and peaceful scene of a slow, summer day. I have spent many days and long hours on this lake. It has become my healing place as it reminds me of the last summer night spent with a man who had come full circle in his life.

This is a new spot to commune with my dad. He is gone from my sight but not my heart. No one else can invade this private moment. The crowds are absent from that summer night not so long ago spent celebrating a wedding anniversary. There is no cake to cut or false smiles to don. I and my dad are together in spirit as I ponder the gift of a life taken by a lie. A lie that created hopelessness and helplessness. A lie he acted upon when he placed the gun to his head.

It's here—in the boat and on the lake—that I begin to see the transformative power of gratitude. It's here where I understand that the power of balance is not in rehearsing what is lost but reciting what remains.

Life tilts are an ongoing tutor that is always on our side. Once we become grateful for the tilt, it loses its power to hold us down and take us under its hypnotic power and control. It cannot crush us, because gratitude invites joy to knock upon a heart that has been sequestered by pain.

Gratitude is a way of seeing a life tilt through a different lens. It creates a vision of hope that life can be renewed and restored, regardless of the tilt experienced. When gratitude is activated by rehearsing what is good and what remains, we're reminded that what was good in life before the tilt remains good now. A beautiful sunset before our tilt is the same beautiful sunset after the tilt. The sweetness of a baby's smile is still sweet. And, the majesty of a mountain range still invokes awe from its onlookers.

Gratitude. Inhale it as medicine to your soul, and exhale it so your heart can remember what is good that remains.

With my dad forever gone, I began to practice gratitude for the gifts he left behind. I could now understand how his life had blessed me, even during the years of his emotional absence. Gratitude allowed me to understand how God used these years as formative in building my character, my worldview, my compassion for the hurting, and in forming my understanding that He is my ultimate source of joy and relational fulfillment.

Practicing gratitude positions us to understand the meaning of the word "enough" and put relational greed where it belongs—in the grave alongside every other idolatrous desire that robs us of our completeness in Christ.

When we're greedy for more love, more time, more personal acknowledgment, more peace and happiness, and more exaltation as a human, we fail to see the gifts that gratitude so willingly brings to our remembrance.

Gratitude will remind us that what we have now is enough to build our lives upon. It tells us that our choices need to be based on what remains after a lift tilt, not on what we lost or wish we could have restored. Gratitude reminds us that we become what we focus upon, as seen in the following story.

THE KEBBITCH ITCH

In this Jewish tale,[1] a woman named Anna Kebbitch, known as a chronic complainer, develops an itch on her nose. Each day, all day long, this woman complains about her poor health and insufficient means to provide for herself. She complains about her lack of money to purchase new clothes, about her back, which she claims feels like a wall of bricks, about her daily walk to draw water, which makes her feet feel like watermelons, about her house that's too small that she can't move around in, and about her now-grown children who don't know her.

This complaining and the chronic itch continue until one day when she visits a rabbi to seek his input about what plagues her daily. Upon hearing her story, the rabbi responds, "Anna, your itch is the Kebbitch Itch—the complainer's itch. Its meaning is this: however you consider yourself, so shall you be."

After her visit to the local rabbi, the woman awakens to find herself dramatically changed. She is covered in old rags, her back has turned into a brick wall, her feet are now watermelons, her house has shrunk so small that her arms stick out from the windows and her legs hang out the front door. In addition to all this, her adult children walk by and, seeing her in this condition, they don't recognize her. Still, her nose continues to itch.

In great despair, the woman recalls the meaning behind the Kebbitch Itch. In a moment of clarity and revelation, she begins to express gratitude for at least having enough money to live fruitfully. Out of this vision of abundance, she begins to give to those who have less. Furthermore, she begins to see how her health is good compared to others her age, that walking to get water every day allows her to behold the beauty of flowers strewn throughout the path, and that she is grateful to have children who are capable of independence.

As gratitude infiltrates the space in her heart where complaining once abided, the little Jewish woman is miraculously cured and her life becomes illuminated with daily glimpses of joy and contentment.

The rabbi, upon retelling her story, tells those who will listen, "May your noses itch forever."

TRUSTING THE HEALER

Gratitude is a way of defining your life rather than allowing your life tilt to do so. It's a mentality that accepts the places we're at in life as being enough. When we live in want of more than what is available to us, we strive after a finish line that can never be reached. This constant striving for more leaves us in despair and eternal discontent as our spirit searches for more.

Parched, we glance over the horizon of life and wonder what we've done wrong. We believe we haven't strived long enough or worked hard enough to find the satisfaction in life that we so desperately desire and strive to achieve. In reality, it's not that we haven't worked hard enough or striven long enough. Our only mistake is in not accepting our life as full of God's mercy, grace, and bounty right where He has placed us—as is. In this moment, we conclude God Himself isn't good or enough.

However, when we practice living with gratitude, we understand God is both good and enough and that He extends His grace and mercy to us through our life tilts.

ONE OF THEM TURNED BACK

Luke chapter 10 provides a wonderful illustration of God's provision through gratitude.

Luke recounts the story of ten lepers, excommunicated, who cry out to Jesus. Jesus, the Son of God, was on His way to Jerusalem. The lepers and Jesus meet. What intersects in this moment when they meet are purpose and need.

The lepers were in need of healing, and Jesus' purpose

was to heal. With voices raised they cry out, "Jesus, Master, have mercy on us!" In that moment, Jesus commands them to present themselves to the priest for cleansing. Acting upon Jesus' word, healing is experienced.

Luke continues the story by writing, "One of them, when he saw that he had been healed, turned back, glorifying God with a loud voice, and he fell on his face at His feet, giving thanks to Him" (Luke 10:15–16).

Luke demonstrates that the leper's gratitude for his physical healing was willingly expressed. However, the emotional and spiritual pain those months, or perhaps years, of being excommunicated from friends and family would not be so quickly wiped away. His life tilt encompassed his entire being, and it would take more than physical healing to regain balance.

This balance would come through relationship, and relationship would come through gratitude. In verse 19, Jesus provides further healing when He declares, "Stand up and go, your faith has made you well."

What was this faith Jesus so boldly declared? The faith of trusting in the Healer for restoration as a whole being in need of spiritual, emotional, and mental balance after a life tilt.

Gratitude cast a vision and opened up life space for a relationship with the Healer. It positions us face-to-face with the intent of our life tilts as seen through His glory.

Kay Arthur, in her account of Geoffrey Bull's prison experience in a Communist Chinese camp, shares the following account from his book, *God Holds the Key*:

I had no Bible in my hand, no watch on my wrist, no pencil or paper in my pocket. There was no real hope of release. There was no real hope of life. There was no real possibility of reunion with those I loved. The only reality was my Lord and Saviour Jesus Christ. Divested of all, He was to become everything to me.[2]

Geoffrey had been tortured, confined, and given only meager provisions. For three years he endured the hate of men who were determined to correct his faulty thinking. He was living in the midst of his biggest life tilt. But gratitude ushered him into the presence of a relationship that positioned him to trust and to find balance in the presence of this Healer, Jesus Christ. He writes:

God makes His children kings and priests, however small the immediate domain. My portion was to be in the contemplation of the Lord of glory in the secret place. To see the King in His beauty must be our one desiring. And if He makes us stand in some obscure and darkened corner of His palace yard, we can be sure He puts us there because from that distinct advantage, we, *with our present stature, will behold Him best whenever He comes passing by.*³

The gift of gratitude's vision arrives when we can see the Healer in the midst of our life tilts and continue to watch for Him as we walk through them.

Gratitude strips away the blinding layers of discontent and greed that complaining erects. Complaining grows legions of reasons to believe there is more to our lives than the present space we inhabit. It demands our attention and allegiance and numbs our memory to the gifts of gratitude.

Complaining is defective, because it relies upon desperation—and nothing grasped in desperate moments has staying power. When our grasp weakens, so does our hope. But when we're grateful, we understand that we're best situated to experience Him in intimate relationship when He passes by our pain. Gratitude allows us to be watchful for His presence, so we, like the lepers, can cry out for the Healer. When our cries are heard, the Healer responds. He comes on His own. His response is pure and His healing lasting.

Gratitude fosters trust. Trust that our life tilts bear the gravity of grounding us to enough. Trust that gratitude unites us to the Healer and that in His presence is all we need for hope, healing, and balance. Gratitude allows us to detach from ourselves and our narrow way of viewing the world and enlarges the resources we have in Christ.

PAIN INTO PURPOSE

As I recall that night on the porch with my father, I recognize that it was enough just to be in his presence. It was enough to know that his love for me in that moment could extinguish years of misplaced hope and desire and relational greed. I did not need the crowds, the cake, the fireworks. I didn't even need the applause of twenty-five years of marital matrimony. I simply needed the presence of my father.

Gratitude allows us to embrace the place we're in. I learned this lesson while spending an hour on a lake. I learned to embrace my position in my life tilt and understand the power of gratitude to heal.

January 13, 2008, I wrote in my journal:

Perhaps he [my dad] had not learned to embrace the place where he was at and look out and enjoy the view. It's in our weakest, most fragile moments when the view is the greatest. Pain, the holy ground of beauty and inspiration. Dad, you missed the view because the experience of your pain stole away the beauty of its truth. You could have finished, had you allowed the truth and beauty of pain to inspire and provide a correct estimate of your journey. Dad, I miss you. I love you. I am indebted to you for having gained this perspective.

Gratitude allows us to view ourselves not as victims or survivors of our circumstances but as transformers who are able to turn our pain into purpose and gratitude into vision. Complaining and grumbling halts creative problem solving, while gratitude allows you to pour your life into something productive. Gratitude redirects your gaze outward. There is more to behold when we look out and not in. Had I been looking inward during the days I spent on the lake, I would have missed the grandeur of the greater vision set before me. Gratitude enlarges the view and diminishes the pain.

If not for gratitude, I would still be tethered to a dark and lonely moment riddled with pain so wrenching it would have ensured the death of my soul. Thankfully, gratitude reminded me I was among the living and not in the casket.

Gratitude doesn't come naturally. It must be cultivated through practice. It's produced when we're willing to give up our perceived right to complain and grumble. We have to, with mindful intention, practice speaking what our tilts counter—thankfulness.

After my own life tilt, I had to learn the power of gratitude by making and following a list of practices that have changed the way I now live my life. Here are some suggestions I would like to share with you:

1. Create space. Schedule time into your calendar to sit in silence. Allow the pain of your tilts to open up margin for gratitude. Rather than focusing on what you have lost, recite and be grateful for that which remains. It's what remains that we're stewards over.

2. Keep a journal. Begin with your lament but end with praise.

3. When stuck in a difficult circumstance or relationship, ask what can be learned and applied to your everyday situations. The loss of my dad opened my eyes to seeing the value of those who are alive. Each day I love with intention, regardless of the love returned. I choose to see that I have an opportunity to build bridges of hope into the daily disappointments and setbacks in other people's lives.

4. Turn your pain into purpose. This is the work of gratitude.

5. Each day, look for the Healer, Jesus, to show Himself. When you see Him, offer praise and thanksgiving, believing that this opens up space for healing to enter and do its transformative work. "The joy of the LORD is your

strength" (Nehemiah 8:10b).

6. Create a gratitude bulletin board. Place it in a central area, where you will see it every day. Invite others to contribute to this board. Place artwork, notes, quotes, and cards received on this board. Review your posts daily and breathe a prayer of thanks as you pass by.

7. Turn your feelings of pain into thoughts of gratefulness. When remembering what has been lost through your life tilt, express an opposing word of gratitude. Each time I feel the sting of my dad's loss, I remind myself how grateful I am for his years of hard work, for being a devoted grandfather to my two beautiful daughters, for loving my husband and contributing to his life, and so much more. As I turn my painful thoughts into grateful moments, it propels me further toward living each day with meaning and purpose.

8. Replace the concept of receiving with giving. Perhaps on the anniversary of your life tilt, instead of expecting others to remember you, remember others. Donate your time, resources, and skills to organizations that give back to those going through their own life tilt. One way I have chosen to give back is to train groups and counselors on depression and suicide. It has become my way of living out purpose through pain.

9. Be creative in how you remember the people and

events of your life tilt. Initially, I turned every picture of my dad over and took down anything that reminded me of him. Although I needed permission to do this as part of my grief, I realized months later that it was actually what was hindering my ability to heal. One by one, I flipped his pictures over and began to offer thanks for the many ways he had offered himself. His picture of him donning the cap of a Shriner reminds me to be grateful for all the children and families that were helped because he transported and signed them up for services they could not have afforded with their own means. Being thankful for this picture enlarged my vision and gave me greater inspiration to live out my purpose.

10. Notice what you have. I can recall the day when I looked around and remembered that my mother was alive, my children were healthy and present, my marriage was intact, and my siblings and nieces and nephews needed me. It was not what I had lost but what I had remaining that would occupy my thoughts and energy. It was in these relationships that I had the privilege to belong and work. I began to see life, because I began to be grateful for what inhabited my life space.

11. Write thank-you notes to people of influence. Thank them for being in your life and specifically name the ways they have enhanced your life and enlarged your

vision for living.

12. Find ways to play every day. The value of play reminds us that joy exists, even in the midst of loss.

Remember that none of these practices are done outside of Christ but in His presence. They require us to look for Him and, like the lepers, cry out for healing. Like He did with the one leper, when we offer gratitude, He will enter into relationship and heal us beyond what our tilt took from us. God inhabits the praises of His people.

Be grateful, become inhabited, and be healed, for this is how the gravity of gratitude will ground you.

Living balanced means turning pain into purpose through the practice of gratitude.

Chapter 9

Hope's Hunger

Hope is being able to see that there is still light despite all the darkness.
Desmond Tutu

FOLDED HANDS, CLOSED EYES

Young, her heart is at peace. She has come to a place where she believes that hope lies in folded hands and closed eyes. Never has she felt so sure that this decision to end her confused and painful existence will finally give her peace. Further, she believes this act will lovingly provide what she believes to be the end of her hunger for peace, comfort, and harmony in her relationship with those she loves.

There is calmness in her hands as she quietly removes the cap. She tips the small bottle she holds so confidently and wonders if the prescribing physician understood he was prescribing her life's end, not ending her nervous stomach.

Green is her favorite color. It cannot be any

coincidence that the caplets that tumble into her palm are green. Another sign to indicate that what she hopes for will be ushered forth. There is no hesitation, no contemplation, no counting the caplets. With what she views as a loving act to all, she downs handfuls of pills until the bottle is empty. She looks at the empty bottle she holds with hope and has no regret.

With poise, she pulls back the covers and slides into the neatly made canopy bed she has slept under each night. But this night is different. Tonight, she believes that hope has finally made its final curtain call. She breathes a sigh of relief.

She remembers how the hands are folded. She's witnessed this position at various occasions. As she recalls the look of serenity upon the faces of those she once held dear, she folds her hands across her chest. With a sense of peace and a heavenly smile, she closes her eyes and waits for her hope to finally become tangible and enter into its promise and its presence.

MISPLACED

Hope—it is the cry of our heart. Each day we hope. We look through tear-saturated hearts and hope that believing in hope will not disappoint us. We crave change. We run after wholeness. We desire to be loved as is. We search out purpose and meaning and the hope that when we die we will have completed our life's calling. We hold hope up against our pain and want to believe that our pain serves a purpose greater than our broken hearts can understand. Surely hope will not prove to be our scorn.

Hope means different things to everyone. Each person who dares hold it out as proof of their effort to take the next and necessary step toward living and dying sees a vision worth holding out and holding onto. Or so we hope.

It matters where this hope is placed. It's the tendency of man to hope in that which is temporal, but when we place our hope in anything that has an expiration date—man, money, and material things—it's hope that has become misplaced, otherwise known as false hope. It is, therefore, misplaced hope that disappoints, which isn't hope at all.

HOPE IN FLAMES

Greyhound racing is a competitive sport in many countries. In order to keep the dogs coursing around the track, an artificial lure is placed before them. In hope of catching this false prize, the dogs pursue the lure with no forethought of the cost to their bodies or their spirits. After all, they are dogs that don't understand hope or the consequence of placing hope in vain pursuits.

Years ago at a track in Florida, the greyhound race was set to begin. The starter's gun went off, and out came the dogs in hot pursuit of a faux rabbit. To the surprise of the racetrack sponsors and workers and all the spectators, the rabbit came to a complete stop and suddenly went up in flames. Later, it was discovered that there was an electrical short in the system that caused the rabbit to short out and self-destruct.

What was even more stunning to those in attendance was the response of the dogs when the object of their hope stopped and disintegrated into ashes and smoke. It was reported that some of the racing dogs stopped and simply laid down on the track. Other dogs, not knowing what to do, ran into a wall and broke ribs, and another dog began to chase his tail. Still others stood and howled in distress. In the end, not one dog completed the race, because the object of their hope went up in smoke.[1]

ANOTHER DAY

Morning dawned. She woke, groggy, and realized with some confusion that what she had placed her hope in had vaporized into another day. With little thought, she rose from her burial bed and proceeded to move through her day, pondering her position in life. She didn't speak about this formal burial of false hope she had performed only hours ago. She's afraid that putting words to her bedside burial will only shatter the false beliefs and hopes her pained loved ones clung to so closely. False hope, she concluded, is better than no hope.

And so life continued for this young teenaged girl. But she began to realize something. And it's something that changed the way she lived the rest of her life.

She realized that her hope resided in a person, not in folded hands and closed eyes. She recalled the character of God that her mother had taught her through story; how God sustained her mother through her childhood poverty and the loss of her father at a young age. She recalled the biblical story of Joseph and how God restored Joseph after he had been betrayed by his brothers and left for dead. Sold into slavery, betrayed, and falsely accused of rape, Joseph, a man scorned, was used by God to spare a nation.

Her heart was tender as she began to understand that God is sovereign over all of her life's pain, sorrow, and difficulties. She began to trust that He could move her life forward, like Joseph, and use her for His glory as He revealed Himself through her life. Yes, God is trustworthy, she concluded, and so she moved through her day, pondering the goodness and compassion of God.

Her hope was in God's character, not an end to her circumstances.

LIFEBLOOD

Hope produces a desire or expectation that things can be different, that where we are in our lives today is not where we will end when our lives are over. Hope is the reason we get up in the morning. We believe there is something in our day that will fulfill our longings and desires, fill the holes within our hearts and deep within our souls. Hope allows us to believe change is possible, regardless of how small our step toward change or how delayed the change is in coming. We hope, because we believe that fairness in life does exist and that we will get justice if we deserve it.

When we stop believing in hope, we become like the greyhounds that day on the track as they watched their hope going up in flames. We, too, despair and languish on our burial beds as we become frenzied and break relationships, splinter our families, and shatter personal dreams, all the while chasing life in an endless circle and going nowhere. If none of the previous mute our pain from living with a hope that failed us, we stand and howl at life and to anyone willing to remain within earshot of our piercing moaning and complaining. We begin to believe that hope is futile and so then is our life.

Our hope can only go up in flames if the object of it is

false, like the lures on the racetrack. We chase after the finite, broken, fallible, and lifeless lure. We believe in its power to satisfy our deepest longings. And as we chase after it, we give up our lifeblood to the false lures, believing they have the ability to transform us. When transformation doesn't happen, we collapse in our spirit, believing transformation isn't possible. This is when hopelessness settles over us like a dark cloud, and we enter into despair.

We were designed to hope, but we were never intended to invest our lifeblood into running after a faux lure. When we do, we find the sacrifice demanding and the result demoralizing and hopeless. False hope is costly, and it demands our life.

Real hope, however, "does not disappoint" (Romans 5:5), because our hope is in a person—God. Isaiah 49:23 states that "no one who hopes in me [God] ever regrets it" (The Message). The secret to living with a hope that sustains through the most difficult of life tilts is based on where we place our focus. Greyhounds focus on a faux lure. Our focus, if properly aligned, will lead us into eternity, where God Himself will reside as the eternal light of hope and promise. God is our end point of hope and Christ is the living lure that ushers us into His presence.

Christ. Our focus. Our living hope. Our life's blood.

ETERNITY, FOCUS, TRIUMPH

Living with a focus on Christ provides us with a long-distance view that ushers us into eternity, where justice will reign, pain will be obliterated, and evil has been defeated. God Himself will be the eternal light and joy, because He makes all things new (Revelation 21).

Eternity reminds us that God is the Potter who can take the broken pieces of our lives and remake us into His priceless treasure. He reminds us that pain is temporary and that life tilts, broken dreams, and betrayed and broken relationships are not our final destination. Eternity abolishes our hopelessness, because we're able to loosen our grip on the powerlessness of the false beliefs, dreams, and goals we have chased.

Eternity becomes the litmus test of our hope. It will reveal if what we hoped in and chased after endures or vaporizes into smoke.

Paul Tripp writes in *Forever, Why You Can't Live without It*, "Eternity reminds believers that this hard moment isn't all there is. It tells us where God is taking His people and His world. Eternity assures us that every dark thing will be defeated. Eternity tells us that God's children will be delivered from everything that is false, unwise, destructive, dangerous, and unholy."[2]

Christ, our Living Hope, and eternity, our promised destination.

When the hope of Christ and eternity become our focus, they can also become our guiding force while in the midst of painful life tilts. This force takes us into the light while in dark moments. Hope reminds us that this light is God, and His life is the eternal torch that directs our destiny. Our delivery from pain may not occur in this life, but with a right focus we can turn our pain into triumph. Why? Because Christ can teach us how to suffer, and in our suffering, He can teach us how to live.

Hope is not about chasing after false beliefs or pursuits. It's about focus. It matters where we place our focus, because hope will follow focus. And if our focus is off, our hope will crumble into shattered spirits.

Focus requires practice. It takes a commitment to refuse the distractions of the world's false lures. We must refuse to hope that people or perfect circumstances will keep us balanced and moving forward. Hope reminds us that forward living in the midst of pain is where triumphal living is experienced.

We can live triumphal in the midst of our pain and grief because we are reminded that pain is normal, but hope is possible. We practice hope by reminding ourselves daily that Christ is our comfort, not man.

Daily we must fan the flames of hope and practice placing our focus on the real and eternal—Christ. God's Word is the tool we need to keep us moving forward in our lives. It is in the daily washing of our minds with His words that we will stay encouraged. God's precious words of hope and encouragement can be found all throughout Scripture.

Jesus said, "I am the bread of life; he who comes to Me will not hunger, and he who believes in Me will never thirst." John 6:35

"Truly, truly, I say to you, he who believes [in Me] has eternal life." John 6:47

"Therefore we do not lose heart, but though our outer man is decaying, yet our inner man is being renewed day by day. For momentary, light affliction is producing for us an eternal weight of glory far beyond all comparison, while we look not at the things which are seen, but at the things which are not seen; for the things which are seen are temporal, but the things which are not seen are eternal." 2 Corinthians 4:16–18

"Things which eye has not seen and ear has not heard, and which have not entered the heart of man, all that God has prepared for those who love Him." 1 Corinthians 2:9

"But in all these things we overwhelmingly conquer through Him who loves us. For I am convinced that neither death, nor life, nor angels, nor principalities, nor things present, nor things to come, nor powers, nor height, nor depth, nor any created thing, will be able to separate us from the love of God, which is in Christ Jesus our Lord." Romans 8:37–39

"This I recall to my mind, therefore I have hope. The Lord's loving kindnesses indeed never cease, for His compassions never fail. They are new every morning; great is Your faithfulness. 'The Lord is my portion,' says my soul, 'Therefore I have hope in Him.' The Lord is good to those who wait for Him, to the person who seeks Him." Lamentations 3:21–25

"The LORD is near to the brokenhearted and saves those who are crushed in spirit." Psalm 34:18

"I will never desert you, nor will I ever forsake you." Hebrews 13:5

The hopes of these promises that come wrapped in Christ are endless. We must not waiver in our commitment to diligently pursue these truths. When we eat at His table, our hope will never again hunger after the false and the futile, because hope's hunger will be satisfied with the promise of forever.

Life tilts remind us what is worth hoping in.

LIVING HOPE

As she looks into his face, she remembers. She recalls the night with shame. She never shared with him about her moment of hopelessness, when she willingly crafted her own casket under her canopy and selected her own burial clothes. His hands are folded in the same manner as hers that night so many, many years ago. *What secrets did he take to his grave?* She ponders. Now she must ask herself if this will be her own secret that she will continue to guard until her children stand over her final casket and muse over their mother's hidden secrets.

What would he think to have known that she understood far more than he ever could have imagined? She wishes she had shared that moment with him in hopes that he could have found a reason to hope for her. Perhaps the sharing would have been a way to purpose in him the hope of assignment. But she didn't tell him, and today she stands looking into the casket she picked for him.

All she can tearfully do is reach down, tenderly kiss his bruised and swollen face, and bid her final, "I love you, Dad." Her hope is now laser-focused as she realizes she will one day reunite with him and share her story of hope and how one misplaced, hopeful evening God spared her life.

She vows to make his hopelessness and consequential

death her mission to a broken and hurting world. She will tell his story, but she will also tell hers.

Her vision? To facilitate healing and wholeness through the hope of God's redemptive love.

Her mission? To passionately and authentically love individuals from all backgrounds as they are and where they are.

Her ministry—my ministry—is "Living Hope Ministries Today."

You see, my dad's story is really mine, because it originally started out one night long ago under the canopy of a teenage girl's bed.

When hope is properly fixed on what is real and living, our life tilts become our assignments. They become the reason we get up in the morning.

It is in Christ that we then understand what 2 Corinthians 1:3 – 4 teaches us about life assignments through life tilts.

Blessed be the God and Father of our Lord Jesus Christ, the Father of mercies and God of all comfort, who comforts us in all our affliction so that we will be able to comfort those who are in any affliction with the comfort with which we ourselves are comforted by God.

The reason I can provide comfort to those who are

under the burden of a life tilt is because Christ, the God of all comfort, has comforted me with the hope of eternity and His abiding love.

Hope's hunger is only found in a person—Jesus Christ, the hope of all eternity.

Living balanced means placing Christ as the object of our hope.

Chapter 10
Living with Vision

The spring will come again, for after winter
there is always spring.
Amy Carmichael

NO TENT

There is a story on the Internet about Sherlock Holmes and Dr. Watson and the time they decided to go on a camping trip. After having dinner and a bottle of wine, they bedded down for the night and went to sleep.

Some hours later, Holmes awoke and nudged his faithful friend. "Watson, look up at the sky and tell me what you see."

Watson replied, "I see millions of stars."

"What does that tell you?" Holmes inquired.

Watson pondered for a minute. "Astronomically, it tells me that there are millions of galaxies and potentially billions of planets. Astrologically, I observe that Saturn is in Leo. Horologically, I deduce that the time is approximately a quarter past three. Theologically, I can see that God is all-powerful and that we are small and insignificant. Meteorologically, I suspect that we will have a beautiful day tomorrow. What does it tell you, Holmes?"

Holmes was silent for a minute, then spoke. "Watson, you idiot. Someone has stolen our tent!"[1]

WAKING UP

Living balanced in a tilted world means we are going to have to allow God to steal our tents of safety and security and predictable outcomes if we're going to understand and experience a greater breadth and depth to our existence and our part in this world. If we want the eyes of our hearts to be opened and our souls enlarged, then we're going to have to trust that the God of this universe steals our life tents that limit our perspective.

When we accept our stolen tent status, we see the purpose behind our life tilts and understand His sovereign plan more clearly. We'll see beauty where barrenness once abided, because this divine act of thievery changes us. At first, we are shocked like Holmes, and perhaps mortified and indignant that our tents of false security and comfort have been removed. But when we can change our focus, like Watson, we can see a greater picture and defining purpose. The temporary comforts we prostrated ourselves before lose their draw upon our hearts and souls.

There is freedom in having our life tents removed. We no longer depend on ourselves to change circumstances, people, or outcomes. Accepting this as an act of providence allows us to see that part of our suffering during our life tilts is due to our limited perspectives. Through life tilts, or stolen tents, God frees us from ourselves and allows us to choose to walk in freedom from thinking we're our own gods.

Laurie Beth Jones, in her book *Jesus Life Coach*, comments after using this same story, "I love the idea of His coming to steal our tent—the tent of our limited perspective, the tent of our fragile and segmented understandings, the tent that we think is keeping us safe, but is really just keeping us from seeing the universe."[2]

Life tilts steal our tents. They challenge us to accept or decline a change in our life, to change our perspective and reorient our relationships with family, friends, and other significant people in our lives. They force us to consider how important it is to be shaken from our world of comfort. Comfort, you see, lulls us into a slumber of the soul. A slumber never grows or expands in its ability to love and console a world filled with different, broken, and hurting people.

I'm not implying our loved ones have no purpose in enhancing and enlarging our capacity to love, nor that the losses we incur are not without pain. When we trust God to use whatever tilts come into our lives to broaden our life view is when we can drink in the beauty and wonder of an all-knowing and all-sufficient God.

Life tilts awaken us to the characteristics of God that are true, sustaining, and life transforming.

Below are a few of the characteristics of God I witnessed after He removed the tent of my limited perspective through my dad's suicide. I documented them in my journal.

Thursday, May 22, 2008 at 7:02 p.m.:

God's sovereignty is complete, because He is a just God, a holy God, a righteous God. I can submit to my circumstance when I understand and accept that the God of all circumstances would not subject me to anything counter to His character.

Through my life tilt, I was able to see that He is sovereign. He assures us that nothing can enter our life without Him overseeing it and using it as the pen that He will use to complete our life stories. God doesn't need erasers, because He writes life purpose with indelible ink, and He uses life tilts as His marking pen to strengthen our life's mission and meaning.

Monday, April 28, 2008 at 6:15 a.m.:

Restore the vision of my life to its proper place. Be thou my vision. Father, God, You chose to purge my soul. The heat of Your love nearly burned my hope, but when hope fainted, Your constant presence controlled my soul's boundaries to understand. Restore hope, renew vision.

He is a provider. Not only will He sovereignly complete our life stories using our life tilts as part of His plan, but He will provide the necessary grace that will sustain us as we submit our tilts to Him. He even instructs us in Matthew 6:11 to pray for "our daily bread." This means that He has manna to sustain us each and every day. We must be willing to focus on the manna He has prepared and not the manna that was stolen. Stolen manna does not sustain. But fresh, daily, holy manna provides.

Monday, May 26, 2008 at 6:58 p.m.:

Today we saw Prince Caspian. *It was very good for many reasons. The kingdom is worth fighting for. It is easy to lose sight of this. I must not lose hope. Realign my vision, Oh Lord, and renew my hope.*

He is a God who sees beyond the boundaries of my limited vision. He knows what lies ahead, and He goes before me to prepare the way. I can trust that His vision is 20/20 and no corrective lenses are needed, except the ones

He lovingly cares to place on me. And we can trust that He acts upon what He sees, although our trust is that He acts according to what is best from His perfect vision and not our limited and distorted understanding.

Tuesday, June 16, 2009 at 12:08 p.m.:

Father, You healed [the] broken, lame man. I, too, have received healing from my brokenness. What did this man do with this gift he had been given? Father, what am I doing with the gift You have given to me? Please allow me, through Your provision and power, to share this gift. Holy God, I submit. Take me. Use me. Here I am.

He is a God who heals. Having our tents stolen or removed forces us to come face-to-face not only with the Creator but the Healer. Having an open view allows us to see that our previously confined view distorted our thinking and created a false sense that we are okay. We are never okay. Sin distorts and wounds. When our tents are removed, God shines His brilliant light upon the sin that has infected and wounded us. We then understand how mortal our wounds are and turn to Him for the healing. We are broken, but He binds our wounds by the very stripes sin inflicted upon Him. (See Isaiah 53:5.) We overcome because our tents were stolen.

DISCOVERING CHANGE

God wants to challenge you to accept His sovereign will to remove your life tent and provide you with greater perspective—one that will enhance you as a human being and foster growth toward expanding your mindfulness of how to live with greater compassion, generosity, and kindness toward humanity.

If we accept this challenge, then we must surrender our default reaction-to-pain buttons and learn to be responsive to pain's lessons. It's comfortable to remain in patterns we know and that have become familiar friends. But in the end, these patterns become the enemy within.

When our tents are removed by life tilts, our eyes are continually on the Lord, if we but open them and see like Watson. Where there is vision, there is a heart in motion. And when the heart is in motion, the feet are sure to follow. Thus, vision provides direction and direction orders our steps, and this is the gift of a life tilt.

Living balanced is also a call to mourn and weep. In so doing, we'll discover how we are changed and made new when we finally see past our tears and sorrow. Living balanced restores our hope that suffering serves a purpose and that this purpose goes beyond our understanding when we submit to God's loving hands of purpose and healing. Living balanced is a call to redirect our gaze from living inward to looking upward to gaze at the beauty that pain can allow us to see.

BUILD LIFE FROM LOSS

Although I have learned to look up and gaze into the radiant face of God, I still miss my dad. I still have moments of sorrow, knowing that he died without having his hope restored. But, in those moments I am also thankful. My life tilt helped me to see the brokenness of the multitudes surrounding me. Had I not had my tent lovingly removed, I would still be small in my understanding of His compassion and my availability to be a conduit of it.

To live balanced in a tilted world is to live mindful of the moment you are in. It is not a desire to turn back the clock of time and rewrite history, for history cannot be rewritten. Rather, history is a lesson for change to be made, and change is made in the present, not in the past. By changing the present, you can influence a future that does not include the mistakes of your past. Being mindful of the present reduces your anxiety over both the past and the future, because it reminds you that you only have the ability to influence this present moment.

Living balanced in a titled world also requires patience. Patience is both a belief and trusting that God will sustain you through your life tilts and deliver His promises on time—not too soon and never too late. It's natural to desire immediate relief from our pain and suffering, but with patience we can act in a manner that will enhance our life's outcomes.

Patience gives us eyes to see the bigger picture of our life tilts. It creates space for us to think creatively through them and balance our way through painful relationships and losses. Patience is the virtue to living balanced.

Living balanced in a tilted world also requires simplicity. This simplicity requests that we believe and trust in God more, and people less. It is not that people are not trustworthy, but we cannot place our trust in man to get us through our life tilts.

Simplicity asks us to let go of commitments that are keeping us overcommitted and off balance. Simplicity also requests that we release relationships that are keeping us off balance. Not every relationship we desire is necessary or helpful. In fact, the relationships we cling to are often the very ones thrusting us off balance and keeping us unstable.

Further, simplicity is a call to accept our losses and learn from them. We need to allow losses to be as is while we move forward in their presence. Loss doesn't hold us back. Rather, our inability to release loss does. Simplicity responds to loss by saying, "Yes, it happened. Now, how can I build a life from this loss that enhances the lives of those around me and in the world?"

It is not the tilt that defines us but what we look at after and during the tilt. I chose to look at Jesus and the cross He bore to heal me and all those who call upon His name. Because of this, I am whole and healed, even though I still cry and hurt. Pain is temporary, but God is eternal, and Christ is my hope, who presents me cleansed and whole.

Your life tilts belong to God. Friend, do you simply *believe* God can carry you across your life tilt or do you trust He can? The difference between the two is the difference between living balanced in a tilted world or stumbling over and crashing. Trust God and Live Balanced in a Tilted World.

Living balanced means allowing God to steal our tents of safety, security, and predictable outcomes.

Epilogue

*Do not seek to efface pain in forgetfulness,
but to elevate it and to dignify it with hope.*
Victor Hugo - *Les Miserable*

Dad, there is not a day I do not think about you. I still hear your final words. I still remember the desperation in which you spoke. But, I am grateful that you loved me enough to pull me into your final moments. Although it was painful, I learned to appreciate the view after the tilt. Our lives were not perfect together, but I have learned that perfect does not exist. I have come to appreciate our imperfect understanding of each other, as it has allowed me to willingly invite other imperfect people to join me in this journey we call life. Because I now understand the importance of imperfect people being allowed to enter my life sphere, I am more grounded, more capable of sharing love, and more willingly to allow the "hurt and dirt" of people's lives to draw near. I now understand it is not me they draw near to, but God. God is love and He died for all the broken, hurting, sin-filled and sin-stained lives, of which I am one of. Together we stand next to the cross on even ground. Thank you, dad, for living and loving and for being imperfect. Because of this, I was able to see Jesus...

"...the author and perfector of my faith who for the joy set before Him endured the cross, despising the shame, and has sat down at the right hand of the throne of God. For consider Him who has endured such hostility by sinners against Him, so that you will not grow weary and lose heart." (Hebrews 12:2-3)

SOURCES

Chapter 1

1. Darleen Zschech, "The Potter's Hand," *Touching Heaven Changing Earth,* 1998.
2. Wayne Rice, *Hot Illustrations for Youth Talks* (El Cajon, CA: Youth Specialties, 1994).
3. Andy Stanley, *When Work and Family Collide: Keeping Your Job from Cheating Your Family* (Colorado Springs: Multnomah, 2011), 88.

Chapter 2

1. Julia H. Johnston, "Grace Greater than Our Sin," 1910.
2. Wayne Rice, *Hot Illustrations for Youth Talks* (El Cajon, CA: Youth Specialties, 1994).

Chapter 3

1. Edward T. Welch, *Depression: Looking Up from the Stubborn Darkness,*(Greensboro: New Growth Press, 2011).
2. Max Lucado, *Just like Jesus (*Nashville: Word, 1998).

Chapter 4

1. Dr. Seuss, *The Sneetches and Other Stories* (New York: Random House, 1961).
2. Dottie Rambo, "Sheltered in the Arms of God."

Chapter 5

1. Luke 12:48.
2. Florence Littauer, "Florence Littauer Quotes," *AZQuotes*, July 2015, http://www.azquotes.com/quote/670238.

Chapter 7

1. Wayne Muller, *A Life of Being, Having, and Doing Enough* (New York: Harmony Books, 2010).
2. Viktor E. Frankl, *Man's Search for Meaning* (Boston: Beacon Press, 2006).

Chapter 8

1. Wayne Rice, *Hot Illustrations for Youth Talks* (El Cajon, CA: Youth Specialties, 1994).
2. Geoffry Bull, *God Holds the Key* (London: Pickering and Inglis, 1978).
3. Kay Arthur, "17." In *Lord, I Want to Know You: A Devotional Study of the Names of God.* (Colorado Springs: WaterBrook Press, 2000).

Chapter 9

1. Wayne Rice, *Hot Illustrations for Youth Talks* (El Cajon, CA: Youth Specialties, 1994).
2. Paul David Tripp, *Forever: Why You Can't Live without It*. (Grand Rapids: Zondervan, 2011).

Chapter 10

1. "Sherlock Holmes and Doctor Watson Go Camping," *Sunny Skyz*, July 2015, http://www.sunnyskyz.com/funny-jokes/20/Sherlock-Holmes-and-Dr-Watson-Go-Camping
2. Laurie Beth Jones, *Jesus, Life Coach: Learn from the Best* (Nashville: Thomas Nelson Publishers, 2004).

Other Books by
Living Hope Ministries Today
These books can be purchased at
livinghopeministriestoday.com

Restored
Healing Prayers and Inspiration
for Those Living with Depression.

Author: Lynne Jordan
ISBN: 978-0-9887651-0-8
$12.99, paperback

Restored was written with the understanding that depression is a disorder of the body, mind, and spirit. Lynne Jordan, author, educator, and nurse beautifully and emphatically enchants readers with prayers that soothe the soul. Whatever your spiritual path, she shows that praying can be a positive supplement to other treatments for depression. Plus, praying may deepen your faith, help you feel less alone, and strengthen your relationship with God.

Journeys
Insights for Daily Living

Author: Lynne Jordan
$9.99, paperback

Journeys is a devotional book that offers perspective. Written from personal life events, Lynne incorporates simple thoughts and ideas to inspire life change and hope. Life is a journey, and each journey has something to impart. Each of us must quiet our hearts and reflect upon the meaning of each moment. Join Lynne and be inspired to find significance in your own life journey.

LYNNE JORDAN, RN, MA, is founder of Living Hope Ministries Today, an organization devoted to sharing the message of hope to individuals navigating mental, emotional, spiritual, and physical challenges. Lynne is also a sought-after speaker, counselor, educator and mentor who works with people both professionally and personally. She has published two books. Lynne's passion is to bring hope, a sense of personal value, and the will to live with purpose to those struggling with pain, loss, grief and disappointment. Living Balanced in a Tilted World appeals directly to those currently enduring pain and those seeking to encourage the hurting.

Grief & Loss
Honest Talks with God

Author: Jane C. Barrick
ISBN: 978-0-9887651-1-5
$12.99, paperback

After the tragic loss of her adult son in 2006, Jane found herself on a dark, life shattering journey. Reality—life would never be the same became Discovery—the feelings of devastation would not last forever. Travel with Jane through every heartbreaking stage of grief and loss one prayer at a time. You will experience her confrontational conversations with God as she travels from darkness into the light of comfort and hope.

Other "F" Words
God Wants You To Know

Author: Jane C. Barrick
ISBN: 978-0-9887651-5-3
$12.99, paperback

If you want to be victorious over your fears, flaws and failures this book is for you. If you desire to live a more meaningful life with a goal to be the best person God created you to be, you will find guidance and direction through the openness shared in this authors life experiences. Our fears, flaws and failures can move you forward or mow you over. Learn how they can change your life when placed in the hands of a loving God.

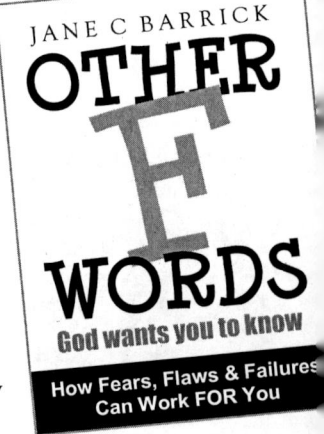

Just Get Me Through the Day!
Inspiration for Surviving Grief, Loss & Other Storms of Life

Author Jane C. Barrick
ISBN: 978-0-9887651-2-2
$12.99, paperback

Jane offers encouragement and inspiration in her personal life stories of God's grace and mercy during grief, loss and other storms of life. These short essays repeatedly demonstrate God's love through His promised resources to endure, survive and recover from heartbreaking life situations. Drawing from her strong faith, personal experiences, and professional knowledge she offers help for fellow travelers experiencing difficult times.

JANE C. BARRICK — As a Social Services professional in Long Term Care for over thirty years, Jane has dealt extensively with individuals experiencing grief and loss. She has lead dozens of Grief & Loss support groups, counseled numerous individuals and completed extensive coursework in the field of Thanatology (the study of death & dying). Seeing life from the perspective of "Christian realism," Jane believes that God is at work in all things while caring about the most intimate details of our lives.